A-Z Street Atlas of NORTHAMPTON & W___ H

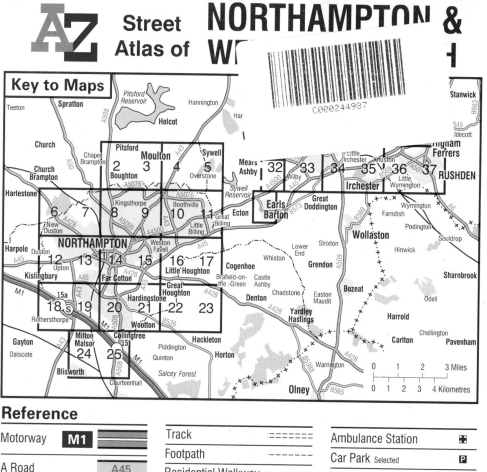

Key to Maps

Reference

Motorway	**M1**	Track	Ambulance Station	✚
A Road	A45	Footpath	Car Park Selected	P
Under Construction		Residential Walkway	Church or Chapel	†
Proposed		Railway — Level Crossing / Station	Fire Station	■
B Road	B526	Built Up Area	Hospital	H
Dual Carriageway		County Boundary	Information Centre	i
One Way Street	→	District Boundary	National Grid Reference	¹45
Traffic flow on A Roads is indicated by a heavy line on the drivers left.		Posttown Boundary — By arrangement with the Post Office	Police Station	▲
Pedestrianized Road	I======I	Postcode Boundary — Within Posttown	Post Office	★
Restricted Access		Map Continuation — 10	Toilet	▽
			Toilet With Facilities for the Disabled	♿

Scale 1:15,840   4 inches to 1 mile

0   ¼   ½   ¾ mile
0   250   500   750   1 kilometre

Geographers' A-Z Map Co. Ltd.

Head Office : Fairfield Road, Borough Green, Sevenoaks, Kent TN15 8PP Telephone 01732 781000

Showrooms : 44 Gray's Inn Road, Holborn, London WC1X 8HX Telephone 0171-242-9246

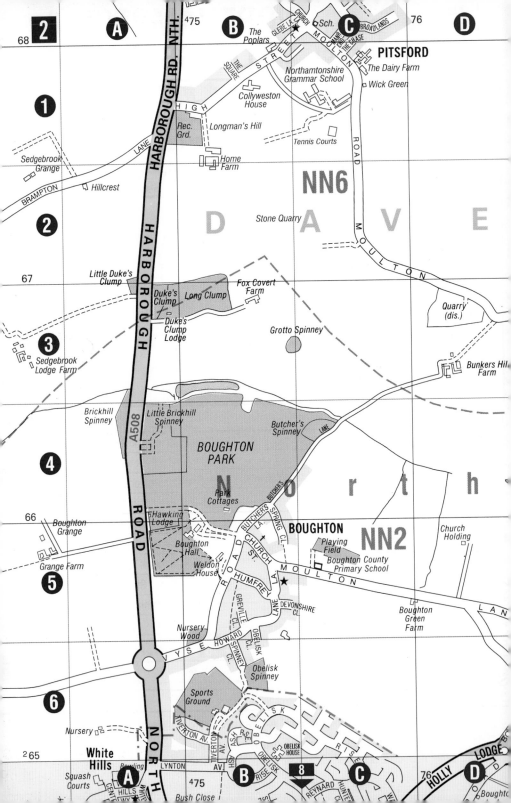

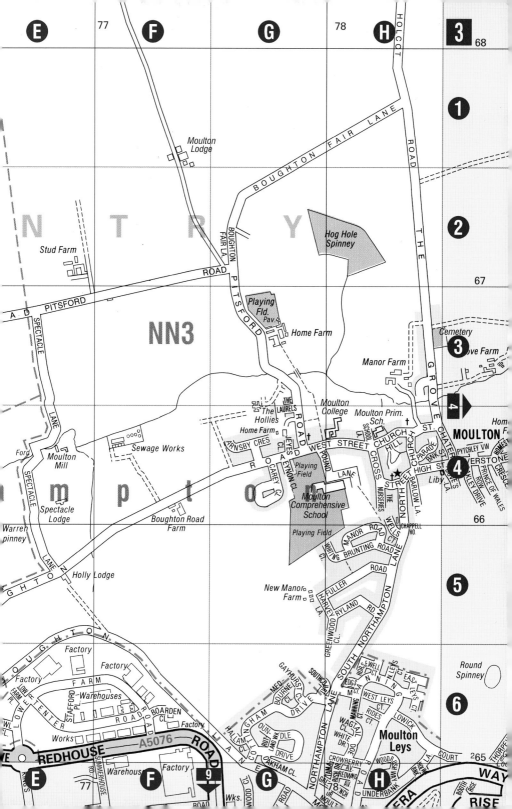

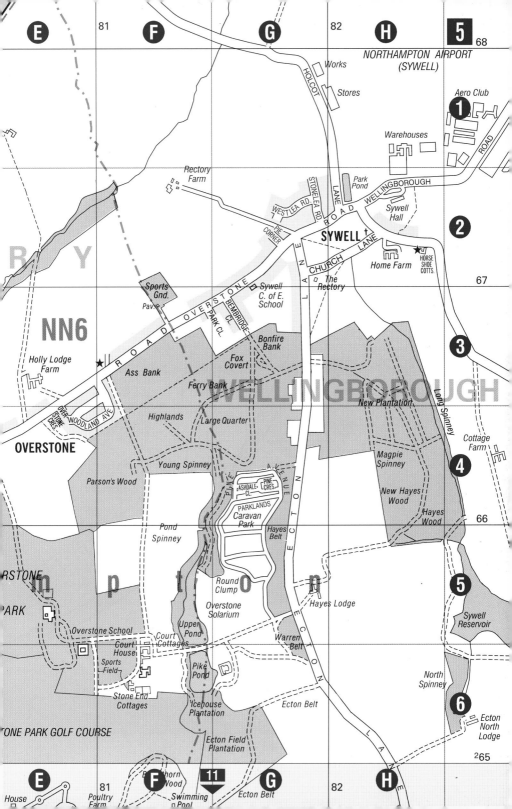

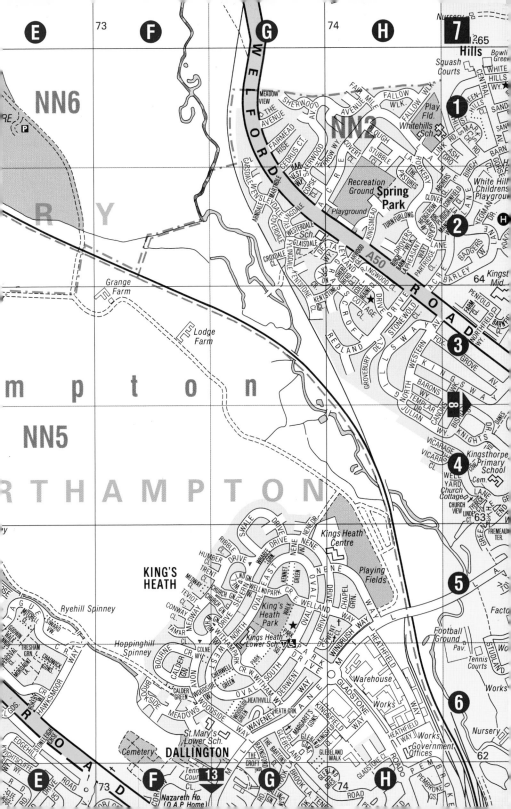

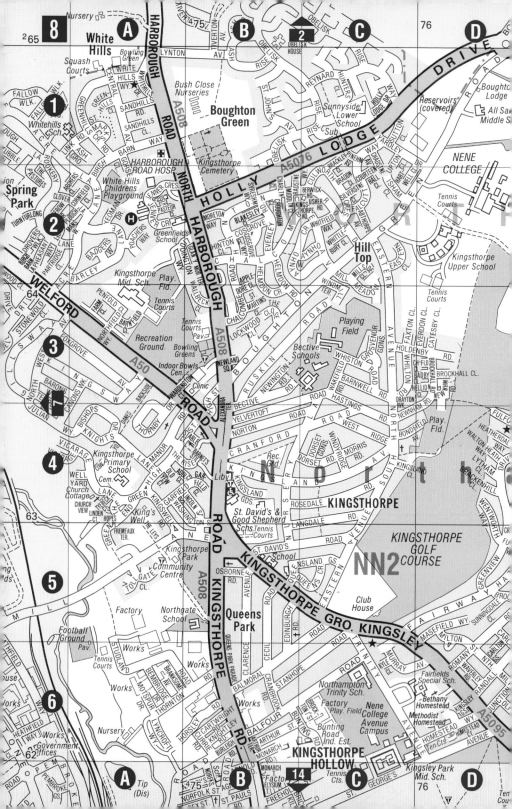

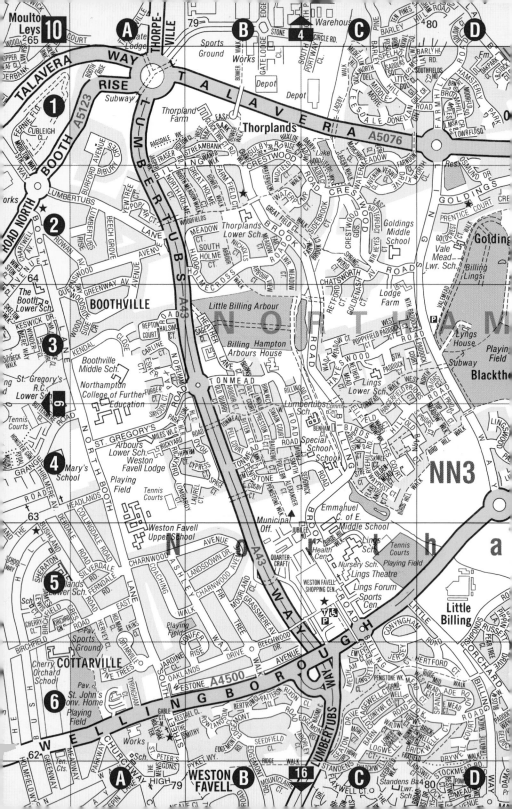

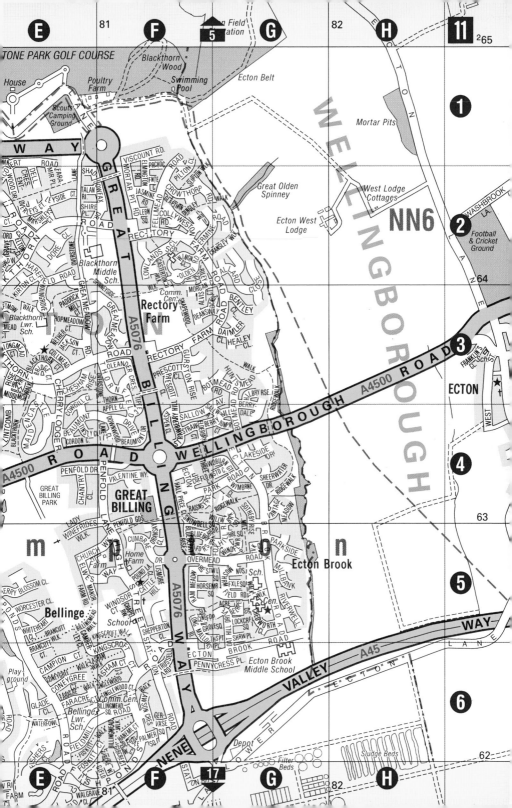

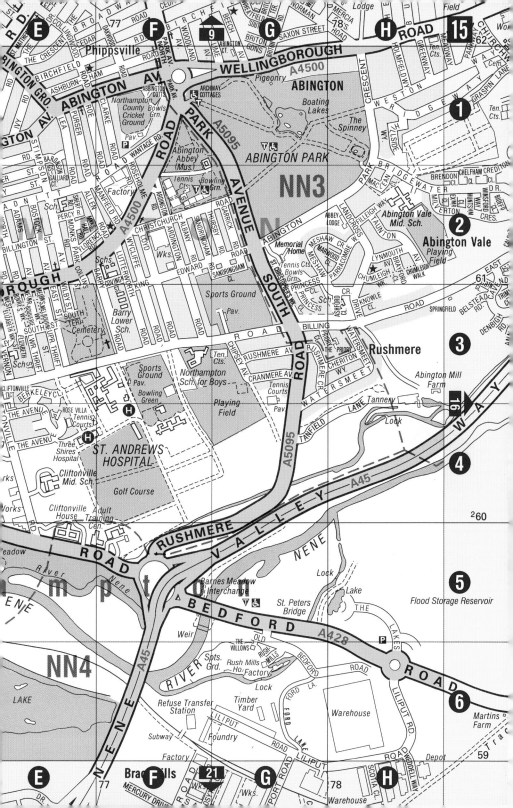

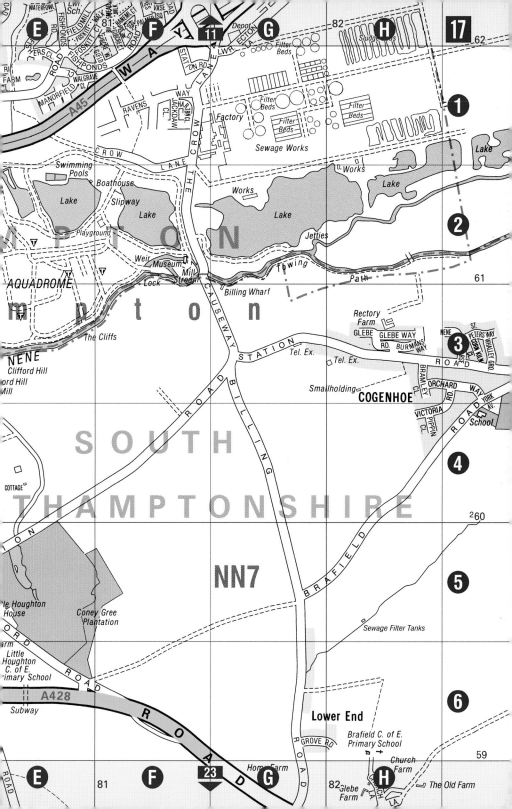

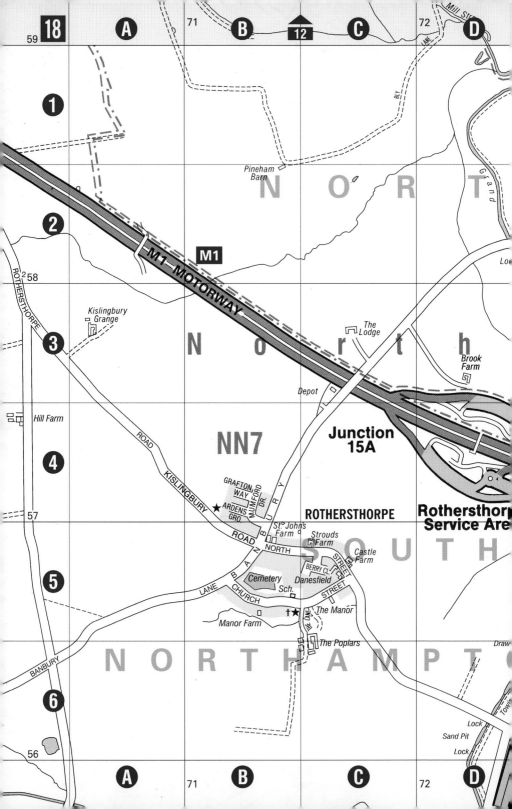

E 77 **F** way **G** LILIPUT 78 **H** RD **21** Martin's Farm 59 Track

Laundry

Factory **15** LILIPUT LANE Depot

Brackmills

MERCURY DRIVE SALTHOUSE ROAD BURRYPORT ROAD SCOTIA CL. DWEDELL WAY

ome arm A45 A-L-L-E-Y DR Wks. OSTH CL. Wks. Warehouse Cycle **1**

RHOSILI ROAD KILVEY CL. Depot PENNARD CL. Depot Cycle ROAD

BRACKMILLS BUS. PK. Wks. Track

RHOSILI ROAD KILVEY CL. OXWICH CL. LYVEDEN RD. GALLOWHILL RD. Works HARROWDN ROAD SKETY CL. ROAD

Works CASWELL Cyclen Track **2**

HILL GOWERTON LOL ²58

HOUGHTON ILEXCL LA. BAXTER CT.

Ivy Ho. Cottage

EET War Meml. The Farm

GROVE THE CONEY GREEN M P T O N ROAD **3**

RUSH RD.

THE WARREN GREEN BACK LA.

RD. THE

DY DR. **22**

THE GREEN Hardingstone Lodge **4**

P A G N E L L Depot 57

HIGH GREEVE GREVE Ridge Farm Factory B526 **NN7 5**

MIDDLE GREEVE LOW GREEVE

New Rectory Farm Rectory Farm

Little Gap Spinney

SOUTH

NORTHAMPTONSHIRE ROAD ange **6**

Grange Cottages 56

E 77 **F** **G** 78 **H** ROAD

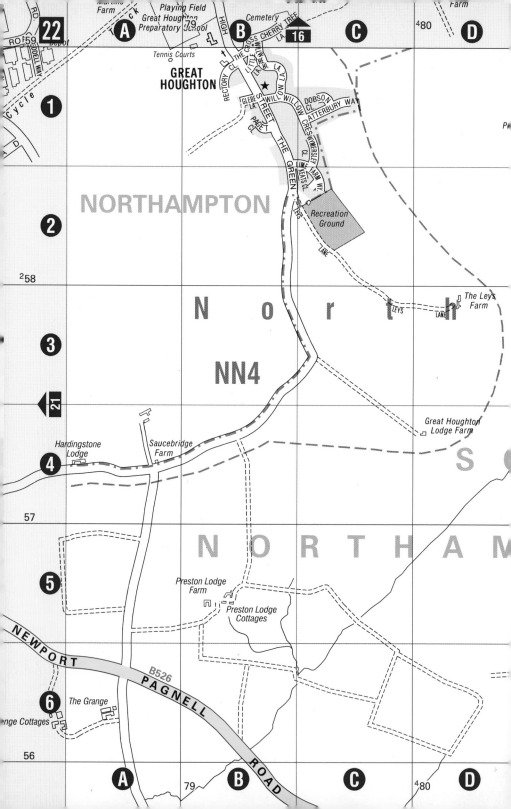

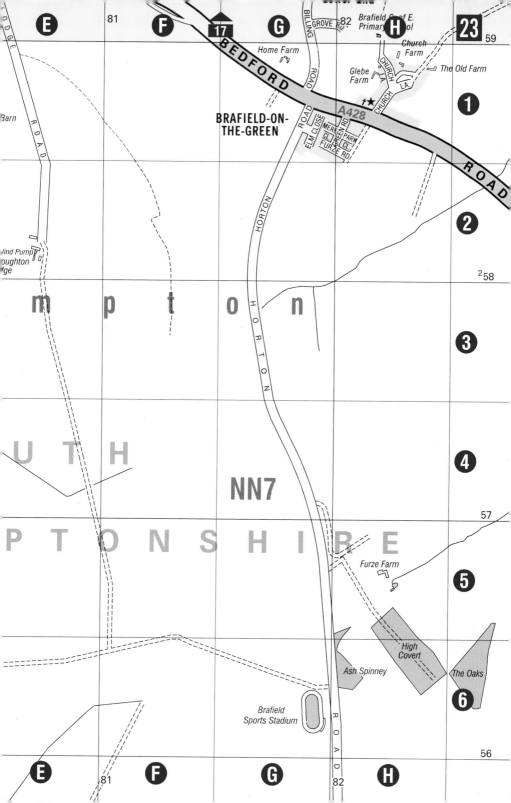

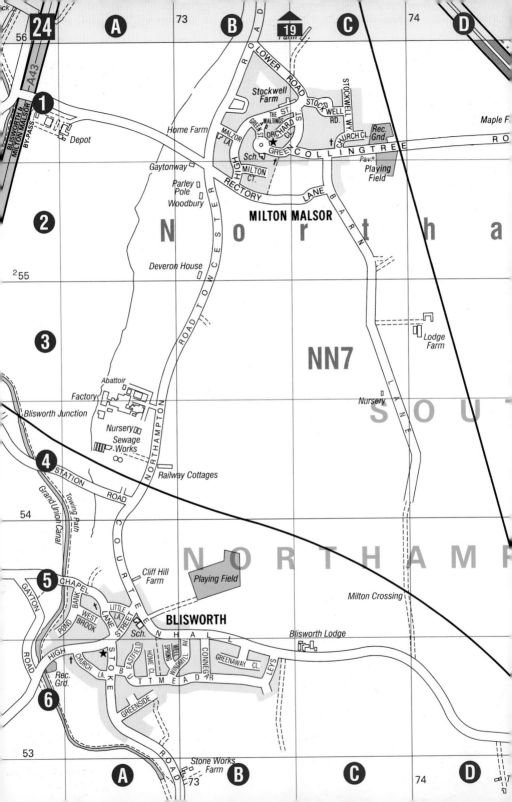

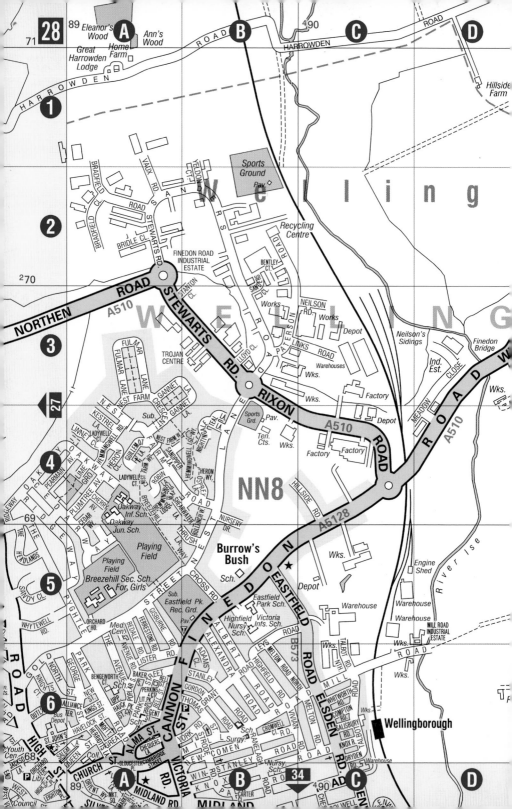

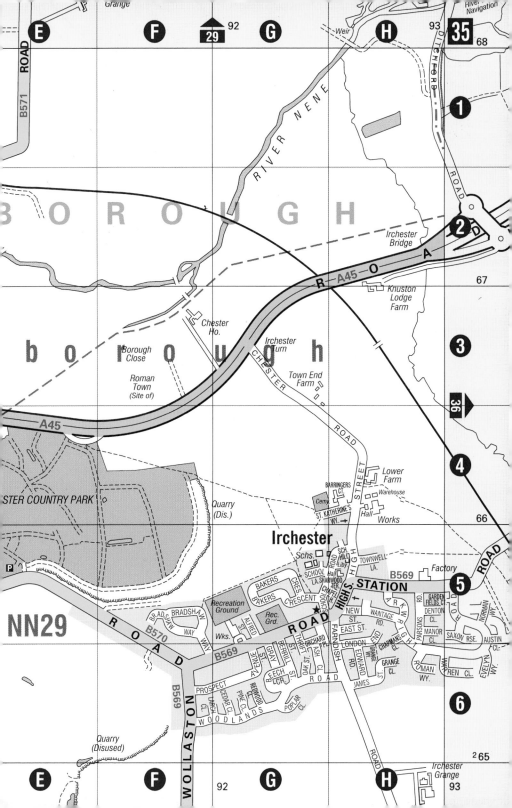

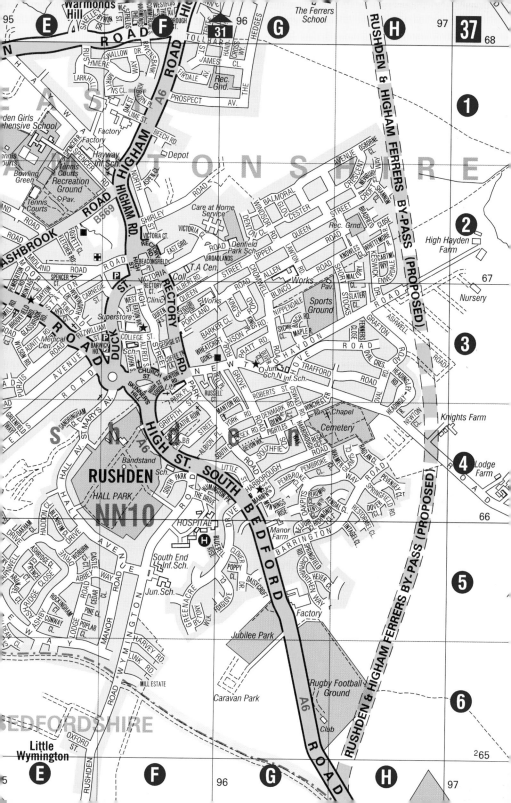

INDEX TO STREETS

HOW TO USE THIS INDEX

1. Each street name is followed by its Postal District and then by its map reference; e.g. Abbey Lodge. NN3 —2H **15** is in the Northampton 3 Postal District and is to be found in square 2H on page **15**.
A strict alphabetical order is followed in which Av., Rd., St., etc. (though abbreviated) are read in full and as part of the street name; e.g. Ashcroft Clo. appears after Ash Clo. but before Ashcroft Gdns.

2. Streets and a selection of Subsidiary names not shown on the Maps, appear in the index in *Italics* with the thoroughfare to which it is connected shown in brackets; e.g. *Adelaide Ter. NN2 —1B 14 (off Barrack Rd.)*

3. With the now general usage of Postcodes for addressing mail, it is not recommended that this index is used for such a purpose.

GENERAL ABBREVIATIONS

All: Alley	Clo: Close	Ind: Industrial	Pl: Place
App: Approach	Comn: Common	Junct: Junction	Rd: Road
Arc: Arcade	Cotts: Cottages	La: Lane	S: South
Av: Avenue	Ct: Court	Lit: Little	Sq: Square
Bk: Back	Cres: Crescent	Lwr: Lower	Sta: Station
Boulevd: Boulevard	Dri: Drive	Mnr: Manor	St: Street
Bri: Bridge	E: East	Mans: Mansions	Ter: Terrace
B'way: Broadway	Embkmt: Embankment	Mkt: Market	Up: Upper
Bldgs: Buildings	Est: Estate	M: Mews	Vs: Villas
Bus: Business	Gdns: Gardens	Mt: Mount	Wlk: Walk
Cen: Centre	Ga: Gate	N: North	W: West
Chu: Church	Gt: Great	Pal: Palace	Yd: Yard
Chyd: Churchyard	Grn: Green	Pde: Parade	
Circ: Circle	Gro: Grove	Pk: Park	
Cir: Circus	Ho: House	Pas: Passage	

INDEX TO STREETS

Abbey Lodge. NN3 —2H **15**
Abbey Rd. NN4 —6A **14**
Abbey Rd. NN8 —3H **33**
Abbey St. NN5 —3H **13**
Abbey Way. NN10 —5E **37**
Abbots Way. NN5 —3G **13**
Abbots Way. NN8 —1H **33**
Abbots Way. NN10 —4D **36**
Aberdare Rd. NN5 —1H **13**
Abington Av. NN1 —1E **15**
Abington Cotts. NN1 —1F **15**
Abington Ct. NN3 —6G **9**
Abington Gro. NN1 —1E **15**
Abington Pk. Cres. NN3 —2G **15**
Abington Pl. NN1 —3D **14**
Abington Sq. NN1 —3C **14**
Abington St. NN1 —3C **14**
Abthorpe Av. NN2 —2C **8**
Acre La. NN2 —2H **7**
Adams Av. NN1 —2E **15**
Adams Clo. NN8 —6B **28**
Addington Rd. NN9 —1D **30**
Addison Rd. NN3 —5F **9**
Addlecroft Clo. NN2 —4A **8**
Adelaide Pl. NN1 —4B **14**
Adelaide St. NN2 —2B **14**
Adelaide Ter. NN2 —1B 14
(off Barrack Rd.)
Adit Wlk. NN3 —2H **15**
Adnitt Rd. NN1 —2E **15**
Adnitt Rd. NN8 —3E **37**
Aggate Way. NN6 —5A **32**
Agnes Rd. NN2 —1B **14**
Ainsdale Clo. NN2 —4E **9**
Aintree Rd. NN3 —3E **9**
Alastor. NN4 —6D **26**
Albany Rd. NN1 —2F **15**
Albert Pl. NN1 —3C **14**
Albert Rd. NN8 —5B **28**
Albert Rd. NN10 —3F **37**
Albion Clo. NN1 —4C **14**
Albion Pl. NN1 —4C **14**
Albion Pl. NN10 —4F **37**
Alcombe Rd. NN1 —2C **14**
Alcombe Ter. NN1 —2D **14**
Alder Ct. NN3 —2C **10**
Alderley Clo. NN5 —1C **12**
Alexander Ct. NN3 —4B **10**
Alexandra Rd. NN1 —3D **14**
Alexandra Rd. NN8 —5B **28**
Alexandra Ter. NN2 —4B **8**
Alfoxden. NN8 —2D **32**
Alfred St. NN1 —3E **15**
Alfred St. NN10 —3F **37**
Alfred St. NN29 —5G **35**
Allan Bank. NN8 —2D **32**

Allard Clo. NN3 —2G **11**
Allebone Rd. NN6 —6B **32**
Allen Rd. NN1 —2E **15**
Allen Rd. NN9 —2C **30**
Allen Rd. NN10 —2G **37**
Alley Yd. NN1 —3B **14**
Alliance Ter. NN8 —6A **28**
Alliston Gdns. NN2 —2B **14**
Alma St. NN5 —3H **13**
Alma St. NN8 —6A **28**
Alpine Rd. NN10 —3D **36**
Alpine Way. NN5 —4B **6**
Alsace Clo. NN5 —6A **6**
Althorp Clo. NN8 —4E **27**
Althorp Rd. NN5 —3H **13**
Althorp St. NN1 —3B **14**
Alton St. NN4 —6A **14**
Alvis Ct. NN3 —3F **11**
Ambleside Clo. NN3 —3H **9**
Ambleside Clo. NN8 —6E **27**
Ambridge Clo. NN4 —3G **19**
Ambush St. NN5 —3A **14**
Anderson Grn. NN8 —1E **33**
Andrew Clo. NN10 —4G **31**
Angel La. NN8 —1A 34
(off Silver St.)
Angel St. NN1 —4B **14**
Anglia Clo. NN3 —1F **9**
Anglia Way. NN3 —1E **9**
Anne Clo. NN10 —4G **31**
Anne Rd. NN8 —3G **33**
Annesley Rd. NN3 —3A **16**
Ansell Way. NN4 —3D **20**
Applebarn Clo. NN4 —1F **25**
Appleby Clo. NN9 —2H **27**
Appleby Wlk. NN3 —3H **9**
Appledore Clo. NN2 —2B **8**
Aquitaine Clo. NN5 —6A **6**
Arbour Ct. NN3 —3B **10**
Arbour View Ct. NN3 —2B **10**
Arbour Wlk. NN3 —2B **10**
Archangel Rd. NN4 —1F **19**
Archangel Sq. NN4 —1G **19**
Archers Clo. NN2 —2A **8**
Archfield. NN8 —1H **33**
Archfield Ter. NN9 —1D 30
(off Lilley Ter.)
Archway Cotts. NN3 —1F **15**
Ardens Gro. NN7 —4B **18**
Ardington Rd. NN1 —2F **15**
Argyle St. NN5 —3G **13**
Ariel Clo. NN5 —6B **6**
Arkwright Rd. NN29 —5H **35**
Arlbury Rd. NN3 —3D **10**
Arndale. NN2 —2G **7**
Arnold Rd. NN2 —1B **14**

Arnsby Cres. NN3 —4G **3**
Arrow Head Rd. NN4 —6G **13**
Arthur St. NN2 —6B **8**
Arthur St. NN8 —1G **33**
Arthur Ter. NN2 —6B **8**
Artizan Rd. NN1 —2E **15**
Arundel Ct. NN10 —5E **37**
Arundel St. NN1 —2B **14**
Ashbrow Rd. NN4 —6G **13**
Ashburnham Rd. NN1 —1E **15**
Ashby Clo. NN8 —4F **27**
Ashby Dri. NN10 —5E **37**
Ashby Rise. NN8 —4G **27**
Ash Clo. NN29 —6G **35**
Ashcroft Clo. NN5 —6C **6**
Ashcroft Gdns. NN3 —5F **9**
Ashdale Clo. NN6 —4G **5**
Ashfield Rd. NN8 —1G **33**
Ashford Clo. NN3 —3H **15**
Ash Gro. NN2 —1A **8**
Ash La. NN4 —1E **25**
Ashley La. NN3 —4A **4**
Ashley Way. NN3 —5A **10**
Ashridge Clo. NN10 —5E **37**
Ash Rise. NN2 —6B **2**
Ash St. NN1 —2B **14**
Ashton Gro. NN8 —3F **27**
Ashtree Way. NN5 —2D **12**
Ashwell Rd. NN10 —3H **37**
Ashwood Rd. NN5 —2D **12**
Askham Av. NN8 —4G **33**
Aspen Clo. NN3 —4F **11**
Aspen Clo. NN10 —2F **37**
Aston Rise. NN5 —1C **12**
Atterbury Way. NN4 —1C **22**
Attlee Clo. NN3 —3G **9**
Attley Ct. NN8 —6E **27**
Augusta Av. NN4 —5A **20**
Austin Clo. NN29 —5A **36**
Austin St. NN1 —2C **14**
Avebury Way. NN4 —3A **20**
Avenue Rd. NN8 —6A **28**
Avenue, The. NN1 —4E **15**
Avenue, The. NN2 —1G **7**
Avenue, The. NN3 —5C **4**
(Moulton)
Avenue, The. NN3 —4F **9**
(Spinney Hill)
Avenue, The. NN5 —2G **13**
Avenue, The. NN8 —6A **28**
Aviemore Gdns. NN4 —2F **19**
Avignon Clo. NN5 —6B **6**
Avon Clo. NN8 —5E **27**
Avon Dri. NN5 —6F **7**
Axehead Rd. NN4 —6G **13**
Aynho Cres. NN2 —2B **8**

Aynho Wlk. NN2 —2C **8**

Back La. NN4 —3E **21**
Badby Clo. NN2 —3D **8**
Badgers Wlk. NN2 —2A **8**
Bailiff St. NN1 —2B **14**
Baird Ct. NN8 —5D **26**
Bakers Cres. NN29 —5G **35**
Baker St. NN2 —1B **14**
Baker St. NN8 —6A **28**
Baker St. NN9 —2C **30**
Bakewell Clo. NN4 —3G **19**
Baldwin Clo. NN3 —3G **9**
Balfour Rd. NN2 —6B **8**
Balham Clo. NN10 —5D **36**
Balmoral Av. NN10 —2G **37**
Balmoral Clo. NN6 —6C **32**
Balmoral Rd. NN2 —6B **8**
Banbury Clo. NN4 —1E **19**
Banbury La. NN7 & NN4 —6A **18**
Bankside. NN2 —4E **9**
Banks, The. NN9 —3H **27**
Bank View. NN4 —4A **20**
Bants La. NN5 —2E **13**
Baring Rd. NN5 —2H **13**
Barker Clo. NN10 —3F **37**
Barker Rd. NN6 —6B **32**
Barley Hill Rd. NN3 —6C **4**
(in two parts)
Barley La. NN2 —2A **8**
Barlow La. NN3 —4H **3**
Barnard Clo. NN5 —1C **12**
Barn Corner. NN4 —1F **25**
Barnet's Stile. NN2 —4B **8**
Barnfield Clo. NN2 —3A **8**
Barnhill Sq. NN3 —1D **10**
Barn La. NN7 —2C **24**
Barn M. NN4 —1F **25**
Barn Owl Clo. NN4 —3H **19**
Barnstaple Clo. NN3 —2B **16**
Barn Way. NN5 —4C **6**
Barnwell Clo. NN8 —5E **37**
Barnwell Dri. NN10 —5E **37**
Barnwell Gdns. NN8 —4F **27**
Barnwell Rd. NN2 —3C **8**
Barnwell Rd. NN8 —4F **27**
Baron Av. NN6 —4C **32**
Baronson Gdns. NN1 —1E **15**
Barons Way. NN2 —3H **7**
Barrack Rd. NN1 & NN2 —2B **14**
Barratt Clo. NN10 —6F **31**
Barret Clo. NN8 —1C **33**
Barringers Ct. NN29 —4H **35**
Barrington Rd. NN10 —5G **37**
Barry Rd. NN1 —2F **15**
Bartons Clo., The. NN5 —6G **7**

Barwick Ho. NN10 —3E **37**
Basil Clo. NN4 —5C **20**
Bassett's Ct. NN8 —1H **33**
Bates Clo. NN10 —6F **31**
Bath St. NN1 —3B **14**
Baukewell Ct. NN3 —4B **10**
Baunhill Clo. NN3 —2A **16**
Baxter Ct. NN4 —3E **21**
Beaconsfield Pl. NN10 —2F **37**
Beaconsfield Ter. NN1 —2C **14**
Beaufort Dri. NN5 —6D **6**
Beaumaris Clo. NN10 —4G **37**
Beaumont Ct. NN1 —3B 14
(off Simon's Wlk.)
Beaumont Dri. NN3 —4E **11**
Beaune Clo. NN5 —6A **6**
Beauvais Ct. NN5 —5A **6**
Beck Ct. NN8 —5F **27**
Becket Way. NN3 —2G **9**
Bective Rd. NN2 —3B **8**
Bedale Rd. NN8 —5A **28**
Bedford Mans. NN1 —4C 14
(off Derngate)
Bedford Pl. NN1 —4C **14**
Bedford Rd. NN1, NN4 & NN7
—4D **14**
Bedford Rd. NN10 —4G **37**
Beech Av. NN3 —5F **9**
Beech Cres. NN29 —6G **35**
Beechcroft Gdns. NN3 —5F **9**
Beech Dri. NN8 —6G **27**
Beech Gro. NN3 —2A **10**
Beech Rd. NN10 —1F **37**
Beechwood Dri. NN3 —5B **10**
Beechwood Rd. NN5 —2D **12**
Beeston Av. NN3 —1C **16**
Belfield Clo. NN3 —4G **9**
Bell Ct. NN8 —6A 28
(off Bell St.)
Bellropes Sq. NN3 —5G **11**
Bell St. NN8 —6A **28**
Belstead Rd. NN3 —3A **16**
Belton Clo. NN4 —3B **20**
Belvedere Clo. NN5 —2G **13**
Belvoir Clo. NN5 —6C **6**
Belvoir Clo. NN10 —5G **37**
Bembridge Clo. NN6 —3G **5**
Bembridge Dri. NN2 —6A **8**
Benedict Clo. NN10 —5D **36**
Bengeworth Ct. NN8 —6A **28**
Benham Ct. NN3 —4C **10**
Benjamin Sq. NN4 —1G **19**
Bentley Clo. NN3 —3G **11**
Bentley Ct. NN8 —2B **28**
Berkeley Clo. NN1 —3E **15**
Berkeley Houses. NN1 —3B 14
(off Horsemarket)
Bern Links. NN4 —6H **13**
Bern Side. NN4 —6H **13**
Berrill St. NN29 —6G **35**
Berry Clo. NN6 —4B **32**
Berry Clo. NN7 —5C **18**
Berrydale. NN3 —3G **11**
Berry La. NN4 —6C **20**
Berrymoor Rd. NN8 —4G **33**
Berrywood Rd. NN5 —1A **12**
Bertrum Clo. NN3 —6B **10**
Berwick Ho. NN2 —2C **8**
Bestwell Ct. NN3 —1D **16**
Betony Wlk. NN10 —5F **37**
Beverley Cres. NN3 —6H **9**
Bewick Rd. NN3 —2B **16**
Bideford Clo. NN3 —2A **16**
Billing Brook Rd. NN3 —2A **10**
Billing La. NN6 & NN3 —5C **4**
Billingmead Sq. NN3 —6F **11**
Billingmead Wlk. NN3 —6F **11**
Billing Rd. NN1 —3D **14**
Billing Rd. NN7 —3G **17**
Billing Rd. E. NN3 —3G **15**
Billington St. NN1 —2E **15**
Bilston Clo. NN10 —5D **36**
Bilton Ct. NN8 —6F **27**
Birchall Rd. NN10 —3D **36**
Birch Barn La. NN2 —2H **7**
Birch Barn Way. NN2 —2A **8**
Birchfield Ct. NN3 —6G **9**

Birchfield Cres. NN3 —5H **9**
Birchfield Rd. NN1 —1E **15**
Birchfield Rd. NN8 —1F **33**
Birchfield Rd. E. NN3 —6F **9**
Birch Rd. NN10 —3G **37**
Birds Hill Rd. NN3 —4C **10**
Birds Hill Wlk. NN3 —5C **10**
(in two parts)
Birkdale Clo. NN2 —4E **9**
Bishops Dri. NN2 —4A **8**
Bitten Ct. NN8 —2D **14**
Blackberry La. NN4 —6G **13**
Blackfriars. NN10 —4D **36**
Black Lion Hill. NN1 —4A **14**
Blackthorn Bri. Ct. NN3 —3E **11**
Blackthorn Rd. NN3 —3E **11**
Blackthorn Wlk. NN3 —4E **11**
Blackwell Hill. NN4 —3G **19**
Blackymore La. NN4 —6C **20**
Bladon Clo. NN3 —2H **9**
Blakesley Clo. NN2 —2B **8**
Blake Wlk. NN10 —6E **31**
Blaydon Wlk. NN8 —4G **27**
Bledlow Rise. NN4 —3G **19**
Blenheim Clo. NN10 —4E **37**
Blenheim Rd. NN4 —1A **20**
Blenheim Rd. NN8 —4F **27**
Blinco Rd. NN10 —3G **37**
Blisworth & Milton Malsor By-Pass.
NN7 & NN4 —1A **24**
Bloomfield Clo. NN10 —3E **37**
Blossac Ct. NN5 —6A **6**
Blossom Way. NN3 —6D **10**
Bluebell Rise. NN10 —5F **37**
Blueberry Rise. NN3 —5F **11**
Bly La. NN5 & NN4 —4C **12**
Boarden Clo. NN3 —6F **3**
Board St. NN9 —1D **30**
Bobtail Ct. NN5 —6D **6**
Bollinger Clo. NN5 —6A **6**
Bondfield Av. NN2 —4C **8**
Booth Dri. NN8 —1C **32**
Booth La. N. NN3 —2H **9**
Booth La. S. NN3 —4A **10**
Booth Meadow Ct. NN3 —2B **10**
Booth Meadow Wlk. NN3 —2A **10**
Booth Rise. NN3 —1H **9**
(in two parts)
Bordeaux Clo. NN5 —6A **6**
Borough Ct. NN10 —6F **31**
Borrowdale Wlk. NN3 —3H **9**
Bostock Av. NN1 —2E **15**
Botmead Rd. NN3 —3F **11**
Boughton Dri. NN10 —5D **36**
Boughton Fair La. NN3 —2G **3**
Boughton Grn. Rd. NN2 —3B **8**
Boughton La. NN3 —6E **3**
Boughton Rd. NN3 —6E **3**
Boundary Av. NN10 —3C **36**
Bourne Clo. NN8 —5E **27**
Bourne Cres. NN5 —6F **7**
Bourton Clo. NN4 —3G **19**
Bouverie Rd. NN4 —3E **21**
Bouverie St. NN1 —3E **15**
Bouverie Wlk. NN1 —3E **15**
Bowden Rd. NN5 —3H **13**
Bower Wlk. NN3 —1B **10**
(in three parts)
Bowmans Clo. NN4 —2E **19**
Bowthorpe Clo. NN3 —3A **16**
Brackenfield Sq. NN3 —6C **4**
Brackenhill Clo. NN2 —4D **8**
Brackley Clo. NN2 —1C **8**
Brackmills Bus. Pk. NN4 —1F **21**
Bradden Clo. NN2 —2C **8**
Bradfield Clo. NN8 —2A **28**
Bradfield Clo. NN10 —2H **37**
Bradfield Rd. NN8 —2A **28**
Bradmoor Clo. NN3 —1E **11**
Bradshaw St. NN1 —3B **14**
Bradshaw Way. NN29 —5F **35**
Braemar Cres. NN4 —3A **20**
Brafield Rd. NN7 —5G **17**
Braid Ct. NN8 —4F **27**
Bramble End. NN4 —3G **19**
Bramcote Dri. NN3 —1C **16**
Bramhall Rise. NN5 —1C **12**
Bramley Clo. NN7 —3H **17**

Bramley Gro. NN3 —5E **11**
Brammar Ho. NN5 —2G **13**
Brampton Clo. NN8 —4F **27**
Brampton La. NN6 —2A **2**
Brampton Wlk. NN3 —2E **9**
Brancutt Ct. NN3 —6E **11**
Brancutt Wlk. NN3 —5E **11**
Branksome Av. NN2 —6A **8**
Brashland Dri. NN4 —5C **20**
Brayford Clo. NN3 —2H **15**
Brecon St. NN5 —1H **13**
Breezehill Way. NN8 —4A **28**
Brendon Clo. NN3 —2H **15**
Brentford. NN8 —6D **26**
Bressingham Gdns. NN4 —4B **20**
Bretton Clo. NN5 —6B **6**
Briar Hill Rd. NN4 —1A **20**
Briar Hill Wlk. NN4 —1A **20**
Briars, The. NN4 —6H **13**
Brickhill Rd. NN8 —1E **33**
Brick Kiln La. NN2 —1B **14**
Brickwell Ct. NN3 —6C **10**
Brickyard. NN3 —1G **9**
Bridge St. NN1 —4B **14**
Bridgewater Dri. NN3 —2H **15**
Bridle Clo. NN8 —2A **28**
Brightwell Wlk. NN9 —3B **30**
Britannia Gdns. NN8 —1C **34**
Briton Gdns. NN3 —6G **9**
Briton Rd. NN3 —6D **4**
Brittons Dri. NN3 —6G **9**
Briton Ter. NN3 —6G **9**
Broadhurst Dri. NN3 —1C **16**
Broadlands. NN6 —1C **2**
Broadlands. NN10 —2F **37**
Broadmead Av. NN3 —5F **9**
Broad St. NN1 —3B **14**
Broad St. NN4 —5B **32**
Broadway. NN1 —6F **9**
Broadway. NN8 —2A **34**
Broadway E. NN3 —6F **9**
Brocade Clo. NN4 —1G **19**
Brockall Clo. NN2 —3D **8**
Brockall Rd. NN2 —3D **8**
Brockton St. NN2 —6C **8**
Brockwood Clo. NN5 —6B **6**
Bromford Clo. NN3 —1D **16**
Brooke Clo. NN8 —6D **26**
Brooke M. NN8 —6D **26**
Brookfield Rd. NN2 —5D **8**
Brookfield Rd. NN10 —3E **37**
Brookland Cres. NN1 —6F **9**
Brookland Rd. NN1 —6E **9**
Brook La. NN5 —1G **13**
Brookside Meadows. NN5 —6F **7**
Brook St. NN1 —2A **14**
Brook St. E. NN8 —1B **34**
Brook St. W. NN8 —1H **33**
Brook Ter. NN9 —1D **30**
Brook Vale. NN8 —4E **33**
Broom Ct. NN4 —6G **13**
Broomhill Cres. NN3 —1D **10**
Brough Clo. NN5 —6A **6**
Broughton Pl. NN3 —4G **9**
Browning Rd. NN8 —1E **33**
Brownlow Ct. NN3 —3B **10**
Browns Way. NN1 —4D **14**
Bruce St. NN5 —3G **13**
Brundall Clo. NN3 —2A **16**
Brunel Clo. NN8 —5D **26**
Brunswick Pl. NN1 —2D **14**
Brunswick Wlk. NN1 —2D 14
(off Brunswick Pl.)
Brunting Rd. NN3 —5H **3**
Bryant Way. NN10 —5F **31**
Buckingham Clo. NN4 —4A **20**\
Buckwell End. NN8 —1H **33**
Buckwell Pl. NN8 —1H **33**
Bullfinch Way. NN8 —5B **28**
Bunting Rd. NN2 —6B **8**
Bunting Rd. Ind. Est. NN2 —6C **8**
Burford Av. NN3 —2A **10**
Burleigh Rd. NN2 —6B **8**
Burmans Way. NN7 —3H **17**
Burns Rd. NN8 —1D **32**
Burns St. NN1 —2D **14**
Burrows Ct. NN3 —3B **10**
Burryport Rd. NN4 —1G **21**

Burwood Rd. NN3 —5G **9**
Burystead Pl. NN8 —1A **34**
Bush Clo. NN8 —6G **27**
Bush Hill. NN3 —6H **9**
Bushland Rd. NN3 —5H **9**
Butcher's La. NN2 —5B **2**
Butlin Ct. NN8 —4C **34**
Buttermere Clo. NN3 —4H **9**
Buttmead. NN7 —6A **24**
Butts Rd. NN4 —5B **20**
Butts Rd. NN8 —4G **33**
Byfield Rd. NN5 —3H **13**
Byron Cres. NN10 —6E **31**
(Higham Ferrers)
Byron Cres. NN10 —3C **36**
(Rushden)
Byron Rd. NN8 —1F **33**
Byron St. NN2 —6E **9**

Caldbeck Wlk. NN3 —3H **9**
Calder Grn. NN5 —6F **7**
(in two parts)
Calstock Clo. NN3 —2A **16**
Camberley Clo. NN3 —5E **11**
Camborne Clo. NN4 —2A **20**
Cambria Cres. NN3 —6H **9**
Cambridge St. NN2 —1B **14**
Cambridge St. NN8 —6A **28**
Camelot Way. NN5 —1B **12**
Cameron Clo. NN3 —6G **9**
Cameron Clo. NN5 —2F **13**
Cameron Cres. NN5 —2F **13**
Cameron Dri. NN5 —2F **13**
Campbell Rd. NN8 —3A **34**
Campbell Sq. NN1 —3B **14**
Campbell St. NN1 —3B **14**
Campbell Sq. NN6 —5A **32**
Campion Ct. NN3 —6E **11**
Camp La. NN4 —6A **12**
Camrose Rd. NN5 —1H **13**
Candleford. NN3 —3E **11**
Cannon St. NN8 —6A **28**
Canonby. NN8 —1E **33**
Canons Wlk. NN2 —4H **7**
Cardigan Clo. NN5 —1G **13**
Cardinal Clo. NN4 —4A **20**
Carey Clo. NN3 —4G **3**
Carey St. NN1 —2D **14**
Carline Ct. NN3 —3A **10**
Carlton Gdns. NN2 —6D **8**
Carlton M. NN10 —6G **31**
Carlton Rd. NN2 —5D **8**
Carlyle Av. NN5 —2F **13**
Carmarthen Way. NN10 —5G **37**
Carnegie St. NN10 —3E **37**
Carrington Gdns. NN3 —1C **16**
Carter Clo. NN8 —1B **34**
Cartmel Pl. NN3 —4G **9**
Cartmel Way. NN10 —2H **37**
Cartwright Rd. NN2 —6B **8**
Casterbridge Ct. NN4 —4D **20**
Casterton Wlk. NN3 —2F **11**
Castilian St. NN1 —4C **14**
Castilian Ter. NN1 —4C **14**
Castle Av. NN5 —1D **12**
Castle Bush. NN5 —1D **12**
Castle Clo. NN5 —1D **12**
Castle Ct. NN10 —5E **37**
Castle Hill. NN1 —3A **14**
Castle La. NN8 —1A **34**
Castle M. NN8 —1B **34**
Castle Rd. NN8 —1B **34**
Castle St. NN1 —3B **14**
Castle St. NN8 —1B **34**
Castle Ter. NN1 —3A **14**
Caswell Rd. NN4 —2F **21**
Catesby Clo. NN2 —3D **8**
Cattle Hill. NN3 —5F **11**
Cattle Mkt. Rd. NN1 —4B **14**
Catton Cres. NN2 —2G **7**
Causeway, The. NN3 & NN7 —2F **17**
Causeway, The. NN4 —6G **13**
Cavendish Dri. NN3 —3A **16**
Cecil Rd. NN2 —6B **8**
Cedar Clo. NN10 —5E **37**
Cedar Clo. NN29 —6G **35**
Cedar Ct. NN5 —2F **13**
Cedar Rd. NN1 —6E **9**

Cedar Rd. E. NN3 —6F **9**
Cedarway. NN8 —4H **27**
Cedar Way. NN10 —4F **31**
Cedrus Ct. NN2 —1G **7**
Celeborn Pl. NN3 —2E **11**
Cemetery La. NN10 —5F **31**
Central Av. NN2 —1A **8**
Central Av. NN8 —3G **33**
Chace Rd. NN8 —1C **34**
Chadstone Av. NN2 —1C **8**
Chadwick Gdns. NN5 —6E **7**
Chaffinch Clo. NN4 —4G **19**
Chalcombe Av. NN2 —2B **8**
Chalcombe Rd. NN2 —3B **8**
Chalk La. NN1 —4A **14**
Chamberlain Av. NN8 —4G **33**
Chamberlain Way. NN10 —6G **31**
Chantry Clo. NN3 —4E **11**
Chapel Grn. NN5 —5H **7**
Chapel Hill. NN29 —5H **35**
Chapel La. NN7 —5A **24**
Chapel Pl. NN1 —3D **14**
Chapel Row. NN3 —5F **11**
Chapmans Clo. NN29 —5H **35**
Chappell Ho. NN3 —5H **3**
Chardonnay Clo. NN5 —5B **6**
Charles Clo. NN10 —4G **31**
Charles Partridge Ct. NN8 —4E **33**
Charles Robinson Ct. NN8 —2G **33**
Charles St. NN1 —2C **14**
Charles St. NN8 —3G **33**
Charlton Clo. NN2 —2B **8**
Charnwood Av. NN3 —5A **10**
Chartwell Av. NN3 —2H **9**
Chase, The. NN6 —1C **2**
Chater St. NN3 —4A **4**
Chatsworth Av. NN3 —2C **10**
Chatsworth Dri. NN8 —4E **27**
Chaucer Rd. NN8 —1E **33**
Chaucer St. NN2 —5E **9**
Cheddar Clo. NN5 —2E **13**
Chedworth Clo. NN3 —5G **11**
Cheese La. NN8 —1A **34**
(off Market St.)
Chelfham Clo. NN3 —2A **16**
Chelveston Rd. NN10 —5H **31**
Chepstow Clo. NN5 —2H **13**
Chepstow Dri. NN8 —4E **27**
Chequers La. NN8 —6A **28**
Cheriton Way. NN1 —3H **15**
Cherry Av. NN8 —4A **28**
Cherry Blossom Clo. NN3 —5E **11**
Cherry Clo. NN3 —5H **9**
Cherry Ct. NN9 —2C **30**
Cherry Lodge Rd. NN3 —3E **11**
Cherry St. NN9 —2C **30**
Cherry Tree La. NN4 —6B **16**
Cherwell Grn. NN5 —6G **7**
Chesham Rise. NN3 —3E **11**
Chester Rd. NN8 —1C **34**
Chester Rd. NN10 —3D **36**
Chester Rd. NN29 —3G **35**
Chestnut Av. NN4 —6C **20**
Chestnut Clo. NN10 —2D **36**
Chestnut Rd. NN3 —6F **9**
Chestnut Ter. NN3 —5F **9**
Chewton Clo. NN5 —2E **13**
Cheyne Wlk. NN1 —4C **14**
Chichele St. NN10 —5G **31**
Chieftan Bus. Pk. NN8 —5C **26**
Chiltern Av. NN5 —1E **13**
Chiltern Clo. NN5 —1E **13**
Chiltern Way. NN5 —1F **13**
Chilwell Ct. NN3 —1C **16**
Chipsey Av. NN3 —1G **15**
Christchurch Rd. NN1 —2F **15**
Chumleigh Wlk. NN3 —2H **15**
(in two parts)
Church Clo. NN7 —1C **24**
Churchfield Clo. NN2 —3D **8**
Church Grn. NN5 —5G **7**
(in two parts)
Church Hall La. NN10 —4D **36**
Church Hill. NN3 —4H **3**
Church Hill. NN4 —6D **20**
Churchill Av. NN3 —3G **9**
Churchill Av. NN8 —4G **27**
Churchill Rd. NN6 —5B **32**

Church La. NN1 —3B **14**
Church La. NN3 —1D **16**
Church La. NN6 —1C **2**
(Pitsford)
Church La. NN6 —2G **5**
(Sywell)
Church La. NN7 —6A **24**
(Blisworth)
Church La. NN7 —1H **23**
(Brafield)
Church La. NN7 —1A **6**
(Harlestone)
Church La. NN8 —4D **32**
Church St. NN2 —5B **2**
Church St. NN3 —4H **3**
Church St. NN7 —5B **18**
Church St. NN8 —1A **34**
Church St. NN9 —1D **30**
Church St. NN10 —3F **37**
Church View. NN2 —4A **8**
Church View. NN4 —6D **20**
Church Wlk. NN3 —5E **11**
Churchway. NN3 —6A **10**
Church Way. NN8 —1A **34**
(off Orient Way)
Cinnamon Clo. NN4 —5C **20**
Circus End. NN5 —6D **6**
Cissbury Rd. NN4 —5G **13**
Clannell Rd. NN4 —3H **19**
Claregate. NN4 —3A **20**
Claremont Ct. NN1 —3B **14**
(off Simon's Wlk.)
Clarence Av. NN2 —6B **8**
Clarence Ct. NN10 —5E **37**
Clare Rd. NN8 —2E **33**
Clare St. NN1 —2C **14**
Clare Wlk. NN10 —6F **31**
Clarke Ct. NN6 —5C **32**
Clarke Rd. NN1 —1F **15**
Claughton Rd. NN4 —6C **14**
Clayfield Clo. NN3 —1G **9**
Claystones. NN4 —1E **19**
Clee Rise. NN5 —1E **13**
Cliftonville. NN1 —4D **14**
Cliftonville Ct. NN1 —3E **15**
Cliftonville Rd. NN1 —3E **15**
Clinton Rd. NN4 —6A **14**
Clipston Field Pl. NN3 —5F **11**
Clipston Way. NN5 —6D **6**
Clock Tower Ct. NN3 —1B **10**
Close, The. NN2 —3B **8**
Close, The. NN9 —2D **30**
Cloutsham St. NN1 —2C **14**
Clover Dri. NN10 —5G **37**
Clover La. NN2 —2H **7**
Coaching Wlk. NN3 —5A **10**
Codlin Clo. NN3 —6D **10**
Coffee Tavern Ct. NN10 —3F **37**
(off High St. Rushden)
Coffee Tavern La. NN10 —3F **37**
Coldstream La. NN4 —3D **20**
Coleraine Clo. NN2 —3H **7**
College Field Clo. NN3 —4F **11**
College St. NN1 —3B **14**
College St. NN8 —1G **33**
College St. NN9 —1C **30**
College St. NN10 —5G **31**
(Higham Ferrers)
College St. NN10 —3F **37**
(Rushden)
College St. M. NN1 —3B **14**
Collingdale Rd. NN3 —4A **10**
Collingtree Rd. NN7 —1C **24**
Collingwood Rd. NN1 —6E **9**
Collins St. NN1 —2E **15**
Collmead Ct. NN3 —3E **11**
Collyweston Rd. NN3 —2F **11**
Colne Way. NN5 —6F **7**
Colonial Dri. NN4 —6B **20**
Colwell Rd. NN8 —1C **34**
Colwyn Rd. NN1 —2D **14**
Commercial St. NN1 —4B **14**
Commercial St. NN10 —6F **31**
Commercial Way. NN8 —1A **34**
Compton Rd. NN8 —6C **28**
Compton St. NN1 —3B **14**
Compton Way. NN6 —6B **32**
Coneygree Ct. NN3 —6E **11**

Coneygreen. NN4 —3E **21**
Coneygree Wlk. NN3 —6E **11**
Coneywell Ct. NN3 —6C **10**
Conifer Rise. NN3 —5B **10**
Coniston Av. NN3 —4G **9**
Coniston Rd. NN8 —6E **27**
Connaught St. NN1 —2C **14**
Connegar Leys. NN7 —6B **24**
Conway Clo. NN5 —5F **7**
Conway Clo. NN8 —5E **27**
Conway Clo. NN10 —5E **37**
Conyngham Rd. NN3 —5C **10**
Co-operative Row. NN10 —4F **37**
Copper Leaf Clo. NN3 —1H **9**
Coppice Dri. NN3 —2F **9**
Copse Clo. NN2 —2G **7**
Corbieres Clo. NN5 —5A **6**
Cordon Clo. NN3 —4E **11**
Cordon Cres. NN6 —5C **32**
Cornfield Clo. NN2 —2A **8**
Cornhill Clo. NN5 —4D **6**
Corn Kiln Clo. NN7 —3H **17**
Corn La. NN8 —1A **34**
Coronation Av. NN10 —4C **36**
Corran Clo. NN5 —1F **13**
Cosgrove Rd. NN2 —2B **8**
Cosgrove Way. NN2 —2B **8**
Cotswold Av. NN5 —1D **12**
Cotswold Ho. NN5 —1D **12**
Cottage Clo. NN2 —3H **7**
Cottage Gdns. NN3 —4D **10**
Cottage, The. NN3 —3B **16**
Cottagewell Ct. NN3 —6C **10**
Cottarville. NN3 —6A **10**
Cottesmore Clo. NN5 —6C **6**
Cottesmore Way. NN8 —1F **33**
Cottingham Dri. NN3 —6G **3**
Cotton End. NN4 —5B **14**
Cottons, The. NN8 —4F **27**
Countess Clo. NN5 —2H **13**
Countess Rd. NN5 —2H **13**
Courteen Hall Clo. NN2 —2C **8**
Courteenhall Rd. NN7 —5A **24**
Court Rd. NN1 —4B **14**
Coverack Clo. NN4 —2A **20**
Coverdale. NN2 —2G **7**
Covert Clo. NN2 —1H **7**
Covington St. NN1 —2F **15**
Cowgill Clo. NN3 —4E **11**
Cowley Clo. NN4 —5C **20**
Cowper Clo. NN9 —2B **30**
Cowper Rd. NN8 —1E **33**
Cowper St. NN1 —2D **14**
Cowper Ter. NN2 —6D **8**
Cow Yd. NN2 —4A **8**
Coxgrove Way. NN2 —2B **8**
Crabb St. NN10 —4F **37**
Crabb Tree Dri. NN3 —6C **4**
Crabtree Clo. NN8 —3H **33**
Cragside. NN8 —5E **27**
Craigie. NN8 —1E **33**
Cranbrook Rd. NN2 —6B **8**
Crane Clo. NN8 —3A **34**
Crane Wlk. NN3 —1B **10**
Cranford Rd. NN2 —4B **8**
Cranmere Av. NN3 —3G **15**
Cransley Wlk. NN3 —2G **11**
Cranstoun St. NN1 —2C **14**
Craven St. NN1 —2C **14**
Crawford Av. NN5 —2F **13**
Crawley Av. NN8 —4F **27**
Crediton Clo. NN3 —2A **16**
Crescent, The. NN1 —1E **15**
Crescent, The. NN3 —4A **4**
Crescent, The. NN10 —3C **36**
Cresswell Rd. NN10 —3D **36**
Crestline Ct. NN3 —2D **10**
Crestwood Gdns. NN3 —2C **10**
Crestwood Rd. NN3 —1B **10**
Cricklade Clo. NN3 —3A **16**
Crickly Cres. NN4 —6F **13**
Crispin St. NN1 —3B **14**
Crocket Clo. NN2 —5D **8**
Croft Clo. NN8 —6E **27**
Crofters Clo. NN4 —4A **20**
Croftmeadow Ct. NN3 —3E **11**
Croft, The. NN5 —6G **7**
Croft Way. NN3 —2H **37**

Cromwell Ct. NN8 —6B **28**
Cromwell Rd. NN10 —2G **37**
Cromwell St. NN1 —2B **14**
Cross Rd. NN8 —5B **28**
Cross St. NN3 —4H **3**
Cross, The. NN4 —6B **16**
Cross Way. NN9 —3B **30**
Crouch Rd. NN9 —2D **30**
Croughton Clo. NN2 —2B **8**
Crowberry Av. NN3 —6H **3**
Crow La. NN3 —1F **17**
Crownsmead. NN4 —2E **19**
Crowthorp Rd. NN3 —2F **11**
Croxdale Clo. NN2 —2G **7**
Croyland Rd. NN8 —1G **33**
Cubleigh Clo. NN3 —1H **9**
Cullahill Ct. NN4 —1F **19**
Culworth Cres. NN2 —2C **8**
Cumberland Clo. NN3 —4F **9**
Cumbrae Dri. NN3 —5F **11**
Cunningham Clo. NN10 —6F **31**
Currie Rd. NN2 —6B **8**
Curtis M. NN8 —4E **27**
Cypress Ct. NN3 —4B **10**
Cyril St. NN1 —3D **14**

Daimler Clo. NN3 —3G **11**
Dairymeadow Ct. NN3 —1C **10**
Daisy Croft. NN10 —5G **37**
Dale Av. NN8 —6E **27**
Dale Clo. NN8 —6E **27**
Dale Ho. NN8 —1H **33**
(off Hill St.)
Dale Ho. NN8 —1H **33**
(off Wood St.)
Dalestones. NN4 —1E **19**
Dale St. NN8 —1H **33**
Dale, The. NN8 —6E **27**
Dalkeith Rd. NN8 —4H **33**
Dallington Ct. NN5 —1G **13**
Dallington Grn. NN5 —1G **13**
Dallington Haven. NN5 —1G **13**
Dallington Pk. Rd. NN5 —1G **13**
Dallington Rd. NN5 —1G **13**
Dalston Wlk. NN3 —3H **9**
Damson Dell. NN3 —1D **16**
Danefield Rd. NN3 —5G **9**
Dane Ridge. NN5 —3D **12**
Danes Backside. NN2 —4A **8**
Danes Camp Way. NN4 —1E **19**
Danetree Gdns. NN3 —5G **9**
Danewood Gdns. NN3 —5G **9**
Daniels Rd. NN8 —4C **34**
Darby Clo. NN8 —6C **26**
Dark La. NN9 —1F **27**
Darwin Wlk. NN5 —6D **6**
Davy Clo. NN8 —5C **26**
Dayrell Rd. NN4 —1F **19**
Dayrell Sq. NN4 —1G **19**
Dayrell Wlk. NN4 —1G **19**
Dayton St. NN10 —3E **37**
Deacons Ct. NN3 —3F **11**
Deal Ct. NN1 —2C **14**
Deal St. NN1 —2B **14**
Dean Clo. NN10 —5E **37**
Deancourt Dri. NN5 —6B **6**
Deansway. NN3 —3F **11**
Debdale Rd. NN3 —4H **9**
Debdale Rd. NN8 —6G **27**
Deer Pk. Rd. NN3 —1F **9**
Delamere Rd. NN4 —2B **20**
Delapre Cres. NN4 —1B **20**
Delapre Cres. NN4 —6B **14**
Delapre Cres. Rd. NN4 —6A **14**
Delapre St. NN4 —6A **14**
Dell Cres. NN3 —2E **11**
Dell Pl. NN10 —3G **37**
Delta Way. NN2 —2G **7**
Denbigh Rd. NN3 —3A **16**
Denby Dale. NN8 —4F **27**
Dene Clo. NN8 —5F **27**
Denford Way. NN8 —4F **27**
Denington Ct. NN8 —3A **34**
Denington Rd. NN8 —3A **34**
Denington Ind. Est. NN8 —3B **34**
Denmark Ct. NN10 —4G **37**
Denmark Rd. NN1 —3D **14**

Denmark Rd. NN10 —4G **37**
Denton Clo. NN10 —2G **37**
Denton Clo. NN29 —5H **35**
Derby Rd. NN1 —2D **14**
Derngate. NN1 —4C **14**
Derwent Clo. NN5 —5H **7**
Derwent Clo. NN8 —5E **27**
Derwent Dri. NN5 —6G **7**
Devonshire Clo. NN2 —5B **2**
Devonshire Clo. NN8 —5G **27**
Devon Wlk. NN10 —4G **37**
Devon Way. NN3 —2F **9**
Diamond Dri. NN9 —3B **30**
Dianan Ho. NN8 —6F **27**
Dickson Clo. NN4 —6G **13**
Dimock Sq. NN4 —1G **19**
Dingle Rd. NN10 —3B **36**
Dingley Wlk. NN3 —2F **11**
Ditchford Rd. NN8 —4H **29**
Dobson Clo. NN4 —1C **22**
Doddington Rd. NN6 —5C **32**
Doddington Rd. NN8 —5H **33**
  (Wellingborough)
Doddington Rd. NN8 —5D **32**
  (Wilby)
Doddridge St. NN1 —4B **14**
Donellan Grn. NN3 —1C **10**
Donovan Ct. NN3 —1B **16**
Dorchester Ct. NN5 —5B **6**
Dore Clo. NN3 —2E **11**
Dorset Gdns. NN4 —2C **8**
Dorset Rd. NN2 —4C **8**
Douglas Rd. NN3 —1A **10**
Dover Clo. NN10 —4H **37**
Dove's La. NN3 —4A **4**
Downs, The. NN9 —2G **27**
Downsway. NN4 —5A **20**
Downthorpe Hill. NN6 —6B **32**
Downwood Clo. NN3 —4F **11**
Dowthorpe End. NN6 —5B **32**
Drapery, The. NN1 —3B **14**
Draycott Clo. NN3 —2A **16**
Drayton Clo. NN3 —5E **37**
Drayton Pl. NN9 —1D **30**
Drayton Rd. NN9 —1D **30**
Drayton Wlk. NN2 —3C **8**
Drive, The. NN1 —6F **9**
Drive, The. NN5 —2B **12**
Drive, The. NN8 —2A **34**
Drive, The. NN10 —4F **37**
Drovers Wlk. NN2 —2H **7**
Druids Way. NN3 —2E **9**
Drum La. NN1 —3B **14**
Drydale Av. NN3 —4G **9**
Dryden Rd. NN5 —2G **13**
Dryden Rd. NN8 —6C **28**
Dryden Way. NN10 —6E **31**
Dryland Rd. NN3 —5H **9**
Dryleys Ct. NN3 —2E **11**
Drywell Ct. NN3 —6D **10**
Duchy Clo. NN10 —6G **31**
Duck St. NN10 —3F **37**
Duckworth Dell. NN3 —1C **10**
Duke St. NN1 —2C **14**
Duke St. NN8 —4G **33**
Dulce Rd. NN5 —1D **12**
Dulley Av. NN8 —4H **33**
Dulverton Rd. NN3 —2A **16**
Duncan Clo. NN2 —6D **2**
Duncan Ct. NN8 —3F **33**
Dundee St. NN5 —3G **13**
Dunster St. NN1 —3C **14**
Duston Mill La. NN5 —5E **13**
Duston Rd. NN5 —2E **13**
Duston Wildes. NN5 —5B **6**
Dybdale Cres. NN8 —6G **27**
Dychurch La. NN1 —3C **14**

Eagle Dri. NN4 —1D **20**
Earl St. NN1 —3C **14**
Eastbank. NN3 —1B **10**
E. Butterfield Ct. NN3 —2C **10**
East Cres. NN10 —3D **36**
Eastern Av. N. NN2 —2C **8**
Eastern Av. S. NN2 —5C **8**
Eastern Clo. NN2 —2C **8**
Eastfield. NN7 —6A **24**

Eastfield Clo. NN5 —6D **6**
Eastfield Rd. NN4 —6B **14**
Eastfield Rd. NN5 —1C **12**
Eastfield Rd. NN8 —5B **28**
Eastfield, Rd. NN9 —1D **30**
East Gro. NN10 —2F **37**
E. Leys Ct. NN3 —6H **3**
E. Mead Ct. NN3 —6D **10**
E. Oval. NN5 —5G **7**
E. Paddock Ct. NN3 —3D **10**
E. Park Pde. NN1 —1E **15**
E. Priors Ct. NN3 —3D **10**
E. Rising. NN4 —4C **20**
East St. NN1 —3E **15**
East St. NN29 —5H **35**
Eaton Rd. NN5 —6B **6**
Eaton Wlk. NN10 —3F **37**
Ebbw Vale Rd. NN9 —2B **30**
Ecton Brook Rd. NN3 —4G **11**
Ecton La. NN6 —3G **5**
Ecton Pk. Rd. NN3 —4F **11**
Ecton St. NN1 —3D **14**
Eden Clo. NN3 —3G **9**
Edgehill Rd. NN5 —6E **7**
Edgemead Clo. NN3 —6B **4**
Edgemont Rd. NN3 —6B **10**
Edges Ct. NN3 —6H **3**
Edinburgh Rd. NN2 —5B **8**
Edinburgh Rd. NN8 —4G **33**
Edith St. NN1 —3D **14**
Edmonds Clo. NN8 —3A **34**
Edward Clo. NN10 —4G **31**
Edwardian Clo. NN4 —4D **20**
Edward Rd. NN29 —6H **35**
Edwards Dri. NN8 —6F **27**
Ekins Clo. NN3 —5A **10**
Eldean Rd. NN5 —6C **6**
Elderberry Ct. NN3 —4F **11**
Elgin St. NN5 —3G **13**
Elizabeth Clo. NN6 —4B **32**
Elizabeth Clo. NN8 —3F **33**
Elizabeth St. NN1 —3E **15**
Elizabeth Wlk. NN1 —3E **15**
Elizabeth Way. NN6 —4A **32**
Elizabeth Way. NN9 —3C **30**
Elizabeth Way. NN10 —3G **31**
Ellan Clo. NN10 —2C **36**
Ellesmere Av. NN5 —2F **13**
Ellfield Ct. NN3 —4C **10**
Elm Clo. NN7 —1G **23**
Elmhurst Av. NN3 —5F **9**
Elmhurst Ct. NN3 —5F **9**
Elmington Rd. NN3 —2F **11**
Elm St. NN1 —2C **14**
Elm St. NN8 —6H **27**
Elm Wlk. NN10 —5F **31**
Elmwood Wlk. NN5 —6B **6**
Elsden Rd. NN8 —6C **28**
Elton Clo. NN3 —2E **11**
Elwes Way. NN3 —5E **11**
Elysium Ter. NN2 —1B **14**
Emley Rd. NN3 —6C **10**
Enfield Clo. NN5 —1A **12**
Ennerdale Av. NN3 —4F **9**
Ennerdale Rd. NN3 —4F **9**
Ennerdale Rd. NN10 —2H **37**
Enterprise Clo. NN8 —5D **26**
Entwood Dri. NN3 —2E **11**
Ermine Rd. NN3 —2F **11**
Esher Ct. NN3 —3A **10**
Eskdale Av. NN3 —4G **9**
Essex Rd. NN10 —4G **37**
Essex St. NN1 —2B **14**
Ethel St. NN1 —3D **14**
Euston Rd. NN4 —6B **14**
Evelyn Way. NN29 —6A **36**
Evenley Rd. NN2 —2B **8**
Evensford Wlk. NN9 —3B **30**
Everdon Clo. NN2 —3D **8**
Everitt Clo. NN8 —3B **34**
Evesham Ct. NN3 —6D **4**
Excalibur Clo. NN8 —2B **12**
Excelsior. NN8 —1D **32**
Excelsior Gdns. NN5 —1B **12**
Exeter Pl. NN1 —2D **14**
Exmoor Clo. NN3 —2A **16**
Express Clo. NN9 —3C **30**
Eynon Clo. NN3 —4G **3**

Fairfield Rd. NN2 —5E **9**
Fairhurst Way. NN6 —5C **32**
Fairmead Cres. NN10 —5D **36**
Fairmead Rise. NN2 —1G **7**
Fair Mile. NN2 —1H **7**
Fairoaks, The. NN3 —1C **16**
Fairway. NN2 —5D **8**
Fairway, The. NN9 —2G **27**
Falconers Rise. NN4 —3H **19**
Falcutt Way. NN2 —2C **8**
Fallowfield. NN9 —3G **27**
Fallow Wlk. NN2 —1H **7**
Faracre Ct. NN3 —6E **11**
Faracre Wlk. NN3 —6E **11**
Faraday Clo. NN8 —5C **26**
Faraday Ct. NN8 —5C **26**
Faramir Pl. NN3 —2E **11**
Faringdon Ct. NN3 —6D **4**
Farmbrook Ct. NN3 —2C **10**
Farm Clo. NN2 —3A **8**
Farmclose Rd. NN4 —5D **20**
Far Meadow Ct. NN3 —2B **10**
Farm Field Ct. NN3 —2B **10**
Farmhill Rd. NN3 —1D **10**
Farndish Rd. NN29 —5H **35**
Farndon Clo. NN3 —1C **10**
Farnham Dri. NN10 —5D **36**
Farnworth Clo. NN5 —6D **6**
Farraxton Sq. NN4 —1F **19**
Favell Way. NN3 —1A **16**
Fawsley Rd. NN4 —1B **20**
Faxfield Wlk. NN3 —6C **10**
Faxton Clo. NN2 —3C **8**
Fellmead Rd. NN3 —2F **11**
Fell Wlk. NN8 —5F **27**
Fengate Clo. NN3 —2F **11**
Fennel Ct. NN4 —6C **20**
Fenners Clo. NN10 —3H **37**
Ferndale Rd. NN3 —5A **10**
Fernie Field. NN3 —1F **15**
Fernie Way. NN8 —1F **33**
Fern Rd. NN10 —2C **36**
Ferrers Clo. NN10 —4G **31**
Ferrestone Rd. NN8 —5A **28**
Fetter St. NN1 —4C **14**
Fieldmill Rd. NN3 —6E **11**
Field Rose Sq. NN3 —5F **11**
Fieldway. NN3 —6G **9**
Fienesgate. NN4 —2E **19**
Fife St. NN5 —2G **13**
Filleigh Way. NN3 —2H **15**
Finedon Rd. NN8 —5B **28**
Finedon Rd. NN9 —1C **30**
Finedon Rd. Ind. Est. NN8 —2B **28**
Firbank Clo. NN3 —1C **16**
Firdale Av. NN10 —1F **37**
Fir Tree Wlk. NN3 —5A **10**
Firsview Dri. NN5 —6C **6**
Fir Tree Wlk. NN3 —5A **10**
Fishers Clo. NN3 —1E **17**
Fishpond Cottage. NN7 —7E **17**
Fishponds Rd. NN3 —5D **10**
Fish St. NN1 —3C **14**
Fitzroy Pl. NN1 —3A **14**
Fitzroy Ter. NN1 —2B **14**
Fitzwilliam St. NN10 —3F **37**
Five Acres Fold. NN4 —6G **13**
Flaxlands Clo. NN4 —4C **10**
Flaxwell Ct. NN3 —1C **16**
Fleetwind Dri. NN4 —4C **20**
Fleming Clo. NN8 —4D **26**
Fletcher Rd. NN10 —2E **37**
Flintcomb Rise. NN3 —4E **11**
Florence Rd. NN1 —2E **15**
Floribunda Dri. NN4 —6G **13**
Ford La. NN4 —6G **15**
Forest Rd. NN4 —6B **14**
Forfar St. NN5 —2G **13**
Fort Pl. NN1 —3A **14**
Foskitt Clo. NN3 —1E **17**
Foskitt Wlk. NN3 —6E **11**
Foundry St. NN1 —4B **14**
Fourth Av. NN8 —2F **33**
Fowey Clo. NN8 —5E **27**
Foxcovert Rd. NN3 —2E **11**
Foxendale Sq. NN3 —5G **11**
Foxford Clo. NN4 —3G **19**
Foxglove Clo. NN10 —5G **37**

Foxgrove Av. NN2 —3H **7**
Fox Hill. NN4 —2B **20**
Foxhill Rd. NN3 —5G **11**
Foxkett Clo. NN10 —2E **37**
Foxwell Sq. NN3 —6C **4**
Foxwood Clo. NN10 —3C **36**
Frances Jetty. NN1 —4B **14**
Franciscan Clo. NN10 —5D **36**
Francis Clo. NN10 —1C **36**
Francis St. NN1 —2B **14**
Franklin Cres. NN5 —2E **13**
Franklin's Clo. NN6 —3H **11**
Franklin St. NN5 —3G **13**
Fraser Rd. NN3 —1A **10**
Freehold St. NN2 —1B **14**
Freeschool St. NN1 —4B **14**
Fremeaux Ter. NN2 —5A **8**
Friars Av. NN4 —2A **20**
Friars Clo. NN4 —2A **20**
Friars Clo. NN8 —2A **34**
Friars Cres. NN4 —2B **20**
Frinton Clo. NN10 —5D **36**
Frosty Hollow. NN4 —5B **20**
Fulford Dri. NN4 —4D **8**
Fulleburn Ct. NN3 —4B **10**
Fuller Rd. NN3 —5H **3**
Pullingdale Rd. NN3 —5G **9**
Fulmar La. NN8 —3A **28**
Furber Ct. NN3 —3A **10**
Furze Ct. NN4 —6H **13**
Furze Rd. NN7 —1G **23**
Furze Wlk. NN2 —5D **8**
Fylingdale. NN2 —2G **7**

Gable Ct. M. NN3 —6A **10**
Gadesby Ct. NN3 —4B **10**
Gainsborough Dri. NN8 —4H **27**
Galahad Ct. NN5 —2B **12**
Galane Clo. NN4 —2E **19**
Gallfield. NN3 —1F **17**
Galliard Ct. NN1 —2E **15**
Gallowhill Rd. NN4 —2G **21**
Gambrel Rd. NN5 —3E **13**
Gannet La. NN8 —3A **28**
Garden Fields Ct. NN29 —5H **35**
Garfield Clo. NN2 —4B **8**
Garfield St. NN2 —4A **8**
Garrick Rd. NN1 —2G **15**
Garsdale. NN2 —2G **7**
Gas St. NN1 —4B **14**
Gatelodge Clo. NN3 —1B **10**
Gawaine Ct. NN5 —2B **12**
Gayhurst Clo. NN3 —6G **3**
Gayton Rd. NN7 —5A **24**
Gedling Clo. NN3 —1C **16**
Geldock Rd. NN3 —6D **10**
George Nut Ct. NN4 —1B **20**
George Row. NN1 —4B **14**
George St. NN8 —6A **28**
George St. NN9 —2C **30**
George St. NN10 —4G **31**
  (Higham Ferrers)
George St. NN10 —3F **37**
  (Rushden)
Gervase St. NN3 —6F **11**
Gibbsacre Ct. NN3 —6F **11**
Gibbsacre Wlk. NN3 —6F **11**
Gifford Ct. NN5 —1D **12**
Gilbey Clo. NN9 —2G **27**
Gillitts Rd. NN8 —2G **33**
Gillsway. NN2 —3H **7**
Gipsy Rd. NN29 —5C **34**
Gisburne Rd. NN8 —5A **28**
Glade Clo. NN3 —6E **11**
Glade, The. NN9 —2G **27**
Gladstone Clo. NN5 —6H **7**
Gladstone Rd. NN5 —6H **7**
Glaisdale Clo. NN2 —2G **7**
Glamis Clo. NN10 —4H **37**
Glan y Mor Ter. NN2 —2B **8**
Glapthorn Wlk. NN3 —2F **11**
Glasgow St. NN5 —2G **13**
Glassbrook Rd. NN10 —3D **36**
Glastonbury Rd. NN4 —2B **30**
Glebe Av. NN4 —3D **20**
Glebe Clo. NN4 —3D **20**
Glebeland Cres. NN5 —1G **13**

Glebeland Gdns. NN5 —6G **7**
Glebeland Rd. NN5 —6G **7**
Glebeland Wlk. NN5 —6G **7**
Glebe La. NN4 —1B **22**
Glebe La. NN6 —1B **2**
Glebe Rd. NN7 —3H **17**
Glebe Way. NN4 —3D **20**
Glebe Way. NN7 —3H **17**
Glendale Ct. NN3 —6F **11**
Glendale Wlk. NN3 —6F **11**
Glenfield Clo. NN10 —2D **36**
Glenville. NN3 —3G **9**
Gloucester Av. NN4 —1A **20**
Gloucester Clo. NN4 —1A **20**
Gloucester Cres. NN4 —1A **20**
Gloucester Cres. NN10 —2G **37**
Gloucester Pl. NN8 —1A **34**
Godwin Wlk. NN5 —5E **7**
Goldcrest Ct. NN3 —2D **10**
Goldenash Ct. NN3 —3C **10**
Goldings Rd. NN3 —2D **10**
Gold Rd. NN8 —6H **27**
Goldsmith Rd. NN4 —1E **33**
Gold St. NN1 —4B **14**
Goodens La. NN29 —6H **33**
Goodwood Av. NN3 —3E **9**
Gordon Rd. NN8 —6B **28**
Gordon St. NN2 —1B **14**
Gordon St. NN10 —3D **36**
Gorse Clo. NN2 —1A **8**
Gorseholm Ct. NN9 —2D **30**
Gosforth. NN3 —1E **33**
Goslar, The. NN8 —2D **32**
Goughs Cotts. NN5 —2D **12**
Gowerton Rd. NN4 —2F **21**
Grafton Clo. NN8 —4F **27**
Grafton Pl. NN1 —2B **14**
Grafton Rd. NN10 —3H **37**
Grafton St. NN1 —2B **14**
Grafton View. NN4 —5D **20**
Grafton Way. NN5 —5C **6**
Grafton Way. NN7 —4B **18**
Granary Ct. NN4 —4B **20**
Granary Rd. NN4 —4B **20**
Grange Av. NN5 —6C **6**
Grange Clo. NN6 —4B **32**
Grange Clo. NN29 —6H **35**
Grange Rd. NN3 —4H **9**
Grange Rd. NN9 —2G **27**
Grangeway. NN10 —5D **36**
Grange Way. NN29 —6H **35**
Grangewood. NN4 —4H **19**
Grant Rd. NN8 —6B **28**
Grasmere Grn. NN8 —1D **32**
Graspin La. NN3 —1A **16**
Grasscroft. NN2 —2H **7**
Grassmere Av. NN3 —5B **10**
Gravely St. NN1 —2D **14**
Gray St. NN1 —2D **14**
Gray St. NN29 —6G **35**
Gt. Billing Pk. NN3 —4E **11**
Gt. Billing Way. NN3 —2F **11**
Gt. Field Ct. NN3 —2B **10**
Gt. Gull Cres. NN3 —1C **10**
Gt. Holme Ct. NN3 —2B **10**
Greatmeadow. NN3 —3F **11**
Greatmeadow Rd. NN3 —3E **11**
Gt. Park St. NN8 —6A **28**
Gt. Russell St. NN1 —3C **14**
Greenacre Dri. NN10 —5F **37**
Greenaway Clo. NN7 —6B **24**
Green Clo. NN8 —4E **27**
Greendale Sq. NN3 —5F **11**
Green End. NN2 —5A **8**
Greenfield Av. NN3 —4F **9**
Greenfield Rd. NN3 —4F **9**
Green Fields. NN4 —6D **20**
Greenfield Way. NN10 —4E **37**
Green Finch Dri. NN3 —1H **9**
Green Glades. NN4 —2F **19**
Greenhills Clo. NN2 —1A **8**
Greenhills Rd. NN2 —1A **8**
Green La. NN4 —2E **19**
(Hunsbury Hill)
Green La. NN4 —6D **20**
(Wootton)
Greenlaw. NN8 —1D **32**

Green Rd. NN7 —1H **23**
Greenside. NN3 —4H **9**
Greenside. NN7 —6A **24**
Green St. NN1 —4A **14**
Green St. NN7 —1B **24**
Green, The. NN1 —4B **14**
Green, The. NN2 —4A **8**
Green, The. NN4 —2B **22**
(Great Houghton)
Green, The. NN4 —3E **21**
(Hardingstone)
Greenview Dri. NN2 —5D **8**
Greenway. NN3 —3A **10**
(Boothville)
Greenway. NN3 —1H **15**
(Weston Favell)
Greenwood Clo. NN3 —5H **3**
Greenwood Rd. NN5 —3H **13**
Greeves Clo. NN5 —6A **6**
Gregory St. NN1 —4B **14**
Grendon Wlk. NN3 —2E **9**
(in two parts)
Gresham Dri. NN4 —1F **19**
Gretton Clo. NN8 —4F **27**
Greville Av. NN3 —3F **9**
Greville Clo. NN2 —5B **2**
Greyfriars. NN1 —3B **14**
Griffith St. NN10 —4F **37**
Grimmer Wlk. NN9 —3B **30**
Grosvenor Gdns. NN2 —3C **8**
Grosvenor Shopping Cen. NN1
—3B **14**
Groundwell Ct. NN3 —6C **10**
Grovebury Dell. NN2 —3H **7**
Grove Rd. NN1 —2D **14**
Grove Rd. NN7 —6G **17**
Grove Rd. NN10 —3G **37**
Grove St. NN8 —1G **33**
Grove St. NN10 —5G **31**
Grove, The. NN3 —3H **3**
Guildhall Rd. NN1 —4C **14**
Guillemot La. NN8 —4A **28**
Gurston Rise. NN3 —3F **11**

Haddon Clo. NN8 —3F **27**
Haddon Clo. NN10 —5E **37**
Haines Rd. NN4 —6B **14**
Hallam Clo. NN3 —6G **3**
Hall Av. NN10 —4E **37**
Hall Clo. NN5 —3D **12**
Hall Piece Clo. NN3 —4F **11**
Halswell Ct. NN3 —3A **10**
Hambledon Rise. NN4 —6F **13**
Hamlet Grn. NN5 —1G **13**
Ham Meadow Dri. NN3 —5F **11**
Hammerstone La. NN4 —6G **13**
Hampton St. NN1 —2A **14**
Hamsterley Pk. NN3 —1D **10**
Handcross Way. NN10 —1G **37**
Handley Clo. NN5 —6B **6**
Hanemill Ct. NN3 —6F **11**
Hangerfield Ct. NN3 —4C **10**
Hanover Ct. NN3 —3E **11**
Harborough Rd. NN2 —2B **8**
Harborough Rd. NN3 —4G **37**
Harborough Rd. N. NN6 & NN2 —2A **2**
Harborough Way. NN10 —4G **37**
Hardingstone La. NN4 —3C **20**
Harding Ter. NN1 —2B **14**
Hardlands Rd. NN5 —1D **12**
(in two parts)
Hardwick Clo. NN8 —6G **27**
Hardwick Rd. NN4 —3B **26**
Hardwick Rd. NN9 & NN8 —3B **26**
Hardy Dri. NN4 —4E **21**
Harebell Sq. NN3 —5G **11**
Harefield Rd. NN3 —2E **11**
Harefoot Clo. NN5 —1C **12**
Harksome Hill. NN4 —1F **19**
Harlestone Clo. NN5 —2G **13**
Harlestone Ho. NN5 —2G **13**
Harlestone Rd. NN7 & NN5 —1A **6**
Harold St. NN1 —3D **14**
Harrier Pk. NN4 —4A **20**
Harrison Clo. NN8 —6F **27**
Harrowden Rd. NN4 —1G **21**

Harrowden Rd. NN8 —3G **27**
Harrowden Rd. NN9 —1G **27**
Harrow Way. NN2 —1G **7**
Hartburn Clo. NN3 —1F **17**
Hartwell Clo. NN2 —2C **8**
Harvest Way. NN2 —2G **7**
Harvey La. NN3 —5G **3**
Harvey Reeves Rd. NN5 —4H **13**
Harvey Rd. NN8 —2G **33**
Harvey Rd. NN10 —6F **37**
Haselrig Sq. NN4 —1G **19**
Hastings Rd. NN2 —3C **8**
Hatfield Clo. NN4 —3B **20**
Hatfield Clo. NN8 —4E **27**
Hatton Av. NN8 —6H **27**
Hatton Clo. NN3 —1F **9**
Hatton Pk. Rd. NN8 —6G **27**
Hatton St. NN8 —5H **27**
Havelock St. NN6 —6A **28**
Haven Clo. NN5 —2H **13**
Hawkridge. NN4 —2G **19**
Hawksbeard Pl. NN3 —5F **11**
Hawkshead. NN8 —2D **32**
Hawksmoor Way. NN5 —6E **7**
Hawks Nest. NN4 —3H **19**
Hawthorn Rd. NN3 —6F **9**
Hawthorns, The. NN10 —5F **31**
Hawthorn Way. NN8 —6G **27**
Haycroft Wlk. NN2 —2H **7**
Haydon Rd. NN10 —3G **37**
Haydown Grn. NN5 —1E **13**
Hayeswood Rd. NN3 —3C **10**
Hay La. NN9 —2C **30**
Hayride, The. NN4 —4H **19**
Hayway. NN9 —2C **30**
Hayway. NN10 —1E **37**
Hazeldene Rd. NN2 —5D **8**
Hazelwood Rd. NN1 —4C **14**
Headingley Rd. NN10 —3H **37**
Headlands, The. NN3 —5H **9**
Headlands, The. NN8 —5H **27**
Healey. NN3 —3G **11**
Hearden Ct. NN8 —2G **33**
H. E. Bates Way. NN10 —3D **36**
Heather Ct. NN4 —1H **19**
Heather Ct. NN10 —3E **37**
Heatherdale Way. NN2 —4D **8**
Heather La. NN3 —3B **10**
Heathfield Way. NN5 —5H **7**
Heath Grn. NN5 —6G **7**
Heath Rise. NN8 —5F **27**
Heathville. NN5 —6G **7**
Hedge End. NN4 —5B **20**
Hedgerow Dri. NN2 —2H **7**
Hedges, The. NN10 —6G **31**
Hedge Way. NN4 —5B **20**
Hellidon Clo. NN2 —3D **8**
Helmdon Cres. NN2 —2B **8**
Helmdon Rd. NN2 —2B **8**
Hembury Pl. NN4 —6G **13**
Hemmingwell Rd. NN8 —4A **28**
Hemmingwell Way. NN8 —4A **28**
Henley Clo. NN8 —5E **27**
Henry St. NN1 —2D **14**
Henshaw Rd. NN8 —2F **33**
Herbert St. NN1 —3B **14**
Hereward Rd. NN4 —1A **20**
Hermitage Way. NN4 —4C **20**
(in two parts)
Hernhill Ct. NN4 —1F **19**
Heron Clo. NN8 —4A **28**
Heronsford. NN4 —3F **19**
Heron Way. NN8 —4B **28**
Herriotts La. NN8 —6A **28**
Hertford Ct. NN3 —6D **10**
Hervey Clo. NN3 —5A **10**
Hervey St. NN1 —2D **14**
Hesperus. NN8 —1D **32**
Hester St. NN2 —1B **14**
Hever Clo. NN10 —5G **37**
Hiawatha. NN8 —1D **32**
Hidcote Clo. NN4 —4B **20**
Higgins Sq. NN4 —1G **19**
Higham Rd. NN8 & NN29 —4B **34**
Higham Rd. NN10 —1F **37**
Highfield Rd. NN1 —6F **9**
Highfield Rd. NN8 —6B **28**
Highfield Rd. NN9 —1D **30**

Highfield Rd. NN10 —4C **36**
High Greeve. NN4 —5F **21**
Highgrove Ct. NN10 —3F **37**
Highlands Av. NN3 —3F **9**
High St. Blisworth, NN7 —6A **24**
High St. Collingtree, NN4 —2F **25**
High St. Earls Barton, NN6 —5B **32**
High St. Great Billing, NN3 —5F **11**
High St. Great Doddington, NN29
—6G **33**
High St. Great Houghton, NN4
—6B **16**
High St. Hardingstone, NN4 —3D **20**
High St. Higham Ferrers, NN10
—6F **31**
High St. Irchester, NN29 —5H **35**
High St. Irthlingborough, NN9 —2C **30**
High St. Kingsthorpe, NN2 —4A **8**
High St. Milton Malsor, NN7 —2B **24**
High St. Moulton, NN3 —4H **3**
High St. Pitsford, NN6 —1B **2**
High St. Pl. NN8 —1H **33**
High St. Rushden, NN10 —2F **37**
High St. S. NN10 —3F **37**
High St. Wellingborough, NN8
—6H **27**
High St. Weston Favell, NN3 —1A **16**
High St. Wootton, NN4 —5C **20**
High View. NN4 —5D **20**
Hilberry Rise. NN3 —3G **11**
Hillary Rd. NN10 —4D **36**
Hill Clo. NN5 —5D **5**
Hillcrest Av. NN3 —4F **9**
Hilldrop Rd. NN4 —4H **19**
Hill Farm Rise. NN4 —4G **19**
Hillside Rd. NN8 —4C **28**
Hillside Way. NN3 —1H **15**
Hill St. NN8 —1H **33**
Hill, The. NN4 —1B **22**
Hind Style. NN10 —6F **31**
Hinton Clo. NN2 —2B **8**
Hinton Rd. NN2 —2B **8**
Hirondelle Ct. NN5 —6A **6**
Hobby Clo. NN4 —3A **20**
Hodnet Clo. NN4 —4B **20**
Holbein Gdns. NN4 —3F **19**
Holcot Clo. NN8 —3G **27**
Holcot La. NN6 —1G **5**
Holcot Rd. NN3 —1H **3**
Holdenby Rd. NN2 —3C **8**
Hollies, The. NN8 —1G **33**
Hollingside Dri. NN2 —4E **9**
Hollow Bank. NN3 —1H **9**
Hollowell Ct. NN8 —1H **33**
Holly Lodge Dri. NN2 —2B **8**
Hollyoak Ter. NN3 —6A **10**
Holly Rd. NN1 —1E **9**
Holly Rd. NN10 —2C **36**
Holman Clo. NN3 —5A **10**
Holme Clo. NN9 —2G **27**
Holmecross Rd. NN3 —2B **10**
Holmfield Way. NN3 —1H **15**
Holmleigh Clo. NN5 —2D **12**
Holmwood Clo. NN5 —6B **6**
Holyrood Rd. NN5 —2G **13**
Home Clo. NN7 —6A **24**
Home Farm Clo. NN3 —1E **17**
Homestead Clo. NN3 —4A **4**
Homestead Ct. NN2 —6D **8**
Homestead Rise. NN4 —5D **20**
Homestead Way. NN2 —6D **8**
Honister Grn. NN3 —4H **9**
Hood St. NN1 —2D **14**
Hopes Pl. NN2 —4A **8**
Hopmeadow Ct. NN3 —3E **11**
Hopping Hill Gdns. NN5 —6E **7**
Hornbeam Clo. NN8 —6G **27**
Hornbeam Ct. NN3 —4A **10**
Hornby Rd. NN6 —4B **32**
Horse Mkt. NN1 —4B **14**
Horsemoor Sq. NN3 —5F **11**
Horse Shoe Cotts. NN6 —2H **5**
Horseshoe St. NN1 —4B **14**
Horsewell Ct. NN3 —6H **3**
Horsley Rd. NN2 —6B **8**
Horton Rd. NN7 —1G **23**
Houghton Hill. NN4 —2E **21**
Hove Rd. NN10 —3G **37**

Howard Ct. NN8 —6B **28**
(off Mill Rd.)
Howard La. NN2 —5B **2**
Hoxton Clo. NN3 —1A **10**
Hoylake. NN8 —4E **27**
Hoylake Dri. NN2 —4E **9**
Hudson Dri. NN4 —2E **19**
Hulme Way. NN8 —4G **27**
Humber Clo. NN5 —5F **7**
Humber Gdns. NN8 —5E **27**
Humfrey La. NN2 —5B **2**
Hunsbarrow Rd. NN4 —5F **13**
Hunsbury Clo. NN4 —2F **19**
Hunsbury Grn. NN4 —1F **19**
Hunsbury Hill Av. NN4 —6F **13**
Hunsbury Hill Rd. NN4 —1F **19**
Hunsbury Wlk. NN4 —6G **13**
Hunslet La. NN4 —2F **19**
Hunters Clo. NN2 —1C **8**
Hunter St. NN1 —2C **14**
Huntsham Clo. NN3 —2A **16**
Huntsmead. NN3 —3G **11**
Huxley Clo. NN8 —1C **32**
Huxloe Rise. NN3 —1B **10**

Ibstock Clo. NN3 —1D **10**
Icknield Dri. NN4 —2F **19**
Ilex Clo. NN4 —2E **21**
Ingleborough Way. NN5 —1D **12**
Inglewood Ct. NN3 —6F **11**
(in two parts)
Irchester Rd. NN10 —3C **36**
Irondale Clo. NN4 —6F **13**
Ironstone La. NN4 —6F **13**
Irthlingborough Rd. NN8 —2B **34**
Isham Clo. NN2 —2C **8**
Ivy Rd. NN1 —1E **15**
Ixworth Clo. NN3 —2C **10**

Jackdaw Clo. NN3 —1F **17**
Jacklin Ct. NN8 —4E **27**
Jackson's La. NN8 —1H **33**
James Lewis Ct. NN3 —5H **9**
James Rd. NN8 —4A **34**
James St. NN29 —6H **35**
Jardine Clo. NN3 —6A **10**
Jarretts Yd. NN4 —5D **20**
Jasmine Rd. NN3 —2F **11**
Jasper Wlk. NN3 —1A **10**
Javelin Clo. NN5 —1D **12**
Jenner Cres. NN2 —2A **8**
Jersey Ct. NN3 —6C **10**
Jeyes Clo. NN3 —4G **3**
Jeyes Jetty. NN1 —4B **14**
Joan Pyel Clo. NN9 —3C **30**
John Pyle Rd. NN9 —2C **30**
John St. NN10 —3F **37**
Joshua Sq. NN4 —1G **19**
Jubilee Clo. NN4 —6G **13**
Jubilee Cres. NN8 —3H **33**
Jubilee Ho. NN3 —5B **10**
Jubilee St. NN9 —1C **30**
Julian Way. NN2 —4H **7**
Junction Rd. NN2 —6D **8**
Juniper Ct. NN3 —4G **11**

Kealdale Rd. NN3 —3F **9**
Keats Clo. NN4 —2C **22**
Keats Rd. NN8 —1F **33**
Keats Way. NN10 —6E **31**
(Higham Ferrers)
Keats Way. NN10 —2C **36**
(Rushden)
Kedleston Clo. NN4 —3B **20**
Kelburn Clo. NN4 —4A **20**
Kelmscott Clo. NN3 —2D **10**
Kelsall Clo. NN5 —1C **12**
Kendal Clo. NN3 —3A **10**
Kendal Clo. NN10 —4H **37**
Kenilworth Clo. NN5 —1C **12**
Kenilworth Clo. NN10 —4G **37**
Kenmuir Av. NN2 —5E **9**
Kenmuir Cres. NN2 —5E **9**
Kenmuir Gdns. NN2 —5E **9**
Kennet Clo. NN8 —5E **27**

Kennet Grn. NN5 —5G **7**
Kensington Clo. NN10 —2C **36**
Kent Clo. NN5 —3D **12**
Kent Rd. NN5 —2B **12**
Kent Rd. NN8 —4H **33**
Kentstone Clo. NN2 —2G **7**
Kerrfield Est. NN5 —2C **12**
Kestrel Clo. NN3 —6A **10**
Kestrel La. NN8 —4A **28**
Keswick. NN8 —6D **26**
Keswick Dri. NN3 —3H **9**
Keswick Dri. NN10 —2H **37**
Kettering Gdns. NN1 —3D **14**
Kettering Rd. NN1, NN2 & NN3
—3D **14**
Kettering Rd. NN3 —5B **4**
Kettering Rd. N. NN3 —3H **9**
Keyham Ct. NN3 —2D **10**
Kilborn Rd. NN8 —5F **27**
Kilburn Clo. NN8 —4G **27**
Kilburn Pl. NN10 —1F **37**
Kilby Clo. NN8 —2G **33**
Kiln Way. NN8 —6F **27**
Kilvey Rd. NN4 —1F **21**
Kimble Clo. NN4 —3A **20**
Kimbolton Rd. NN10 —5G **31**
King Edward Rd. NN1 —2F **15**
Kingfisher Clo. NN4 —4H **19**
King Richard Ct. NN4 —5B **20**
Kings Av. NN10 —4G **31**
Kingscroft Clo. NN3 —6F **11**
Kingscroft Wlk. NN3 —5F **11**
Kingsfield Clo. NN5 —6G **7**
Kingsfield Way. NN5 —6G **7**
Kingsland Av. NN2 —4B **8**
Kingsland Clo. NN2 —4C **8**
Kingsland Gdns. NN2 —4B **8**
Kingsley Gdns. NN2 —6D **8**
Kingsley Pk. Ter. NN2 —6E **9**
Kingsley Rd. NN2 —5C **8**
Kingsmead. NN2 —2H **7**
Kings Meadow La. NN10 —3E **31**
King's Pk. Rd. NN3 —1E **9**
King's Pl. NN10 —3G **37**
King's Rd. NN10 —3G **37**
Kings St. NN8 —6A **28**
Kingsthorpe Gro. NN2 —5B **8**
Kingsthorpe Ho. NN2 —2C **8**
Kingsthorpe Rd. NN2 —5B **8**
King St. NN6 —4B **32**
Kingsway. NN2 —3H **7**
Kingsway. NN8 —2F **33**
Kingswell Rd. NN2 —4A **8**
Kingswell St. NN1 —4B **14**
Kinross Clo. NN3 —3F **9**
Kirkstone Wlk. NN3 —3H **9**
Kirton Clo. NN3 —3E **11**
Kislingbury Rd. NN7 —4A **18**
Kites Clo. NN4 —3H **19**
Knaphill Cres. NN4 —5G **13**
Knightlands Rd. NN9 —1D **30**
Knightley Rd. NN2 —6B **8**
Knighton Clo. NN5 —4B **6**
Knightscliffe Way. NN5 —6E **7**
Knights Ct. NN3 —6E **11**
Knights Ct. NN8 —6H **27**
Knight's La. NN2 —4A **8**
Knowle Clo. NN3 —3H **15**
Knowles Clo. NN10 —2H **37**
Knox Rd. NN8 —1B **34**
Kyoto Clo. NN3 —1E **9**

Laburnum Cres. NN3 —5F **9**
Laceby Wlk. NN3 —1C **10**
Ladder Maker Yd. NN1 —3B **14**
Ladybridge Dri. NN4 —2E **19**
Lady's La. NN1 —3B **14**
Ladywell Ct. NN8 —4A **28**
Lady Winefrides Wlk. NN3 —5E **11**
Lakeside. NN9 —3B **30**
Lakeside Dri. NN4 —4G **11**
Lakes, The. NN4 —5H **15**
Lakeview Grn. NN3 —3H **9**
Lake Wlk. NN4 —1F **25**
Lambrook Dri. NN4 —4B **20**
Lancaster St. NN10 —5G **31**
Lancum Ho. NN8 —6G **27**

Landcross Dri. NN3 —2H **15**
Landor. NN8 —1E **33**
Landsdown Dri. NN3 —5B **10**
Lanercost Wlk. NN3 —3H **9**
Laneside Hollow. NN4 —5B **20**
Lane, The. NN7 —5C **18**
Langdale Rd. NN2 —4C **8**
Langford Dri. NN4 —6C **20**
Langham Pl. NN2 —1B **14**
Langsett Clo. NN3 —6C **10**
Lapstone Ho. NN5 —4H **13**
Lapwing Clo. NN4 —4H **19**
Larch Clo. NN29 —6F **35**
Larch La. NN5 —5B **6**
Larchwood Clo. NN8 —6G **27**
Larkhill. NN10 —1E **37**
Lark Rise. NN3 —3D **10**
Larwood Clo. NN2 —2H **7**
Lasham Ct. NN3 —6F **11**
Lasham Wlk. NN3 —6E **11**
Latymer Ct. NN1 —3B **14**
Launcelot Clo. NN5 —2B **12**
Laurel Ct. NN3 —4B **10**
Laurels, The. NN3 —4G **3**
Laurel Valley. NN4 —1G **25**
Laurence Leyland Comlex. NN8
—1D **34**
Lavant Wlk. NN3 —2E **9**
Lavenham Clo. NN3 —2C **10**
Lawns, The. NN5 —1F **13**
Lawrence Ct. NN1 —2B **14**
Lawson Cres. NN3 —6F **11**
Lawton Rd. NN10 —2G **37**
Laywood Way. NN9 —3C **30**
Leafields. NN3 —1C **16**
Lea Rd. NN1 —1E **15**
Lea Way. NN8 —1F **33**
Leben Sq. NN3 —2F **11**
Ledaig Way. NN3 —3F **9**
Lees St. NN9 —2C **30**
Leicester Pde. NN2 —1B **14**
(off Barrack Rd.)
Leicester St. NN1 —2B **14**
Leicester Ter. NN2 —2B **14**
Leighton Pl. NN8 —1H **33**
Lennox Wlk. NN5 —5E **7**
Leslie Rd. NN2 —2A **14**
Letts Rd. NN4 —6A **14**
Lewis Rd. NN5 —2G **13**
Leyland Dri. NN2 —2H **7**
Leyside Ct. NN3 —2E **11**
Leys La. NN4 —2B **22**
Leys Rd. NN6 —5A **32**
Leys Rd. NN8 —6B **28**
Leys, The. NN2 —5A **8**
Leyswell St. NN3 —1D **16**
Liberty Dri. NN5 —6D **6**
Lichfield Dri. NN4 —4A **20**
Liddington Way. NN2 —2A **8**
Lilac St. NN8 —6G **27**
Liliput Rd. NN4 —6G **15**
Lilley Ter. NN9 —1D **30**
Lime Av. NN3 —6F **9**
Lime Farm Way. NN4 —2C **22**
Limefields Way. NN4 —5C **20**
Lime Gro. NN8 —4A **28**
Limehurst Clo. NN5 —6D **6**
Limehurst Rd. NN5 —1D **12**
Limehurst Sq. NN5 —1D **12**
Limes, The. NN4 —6D **20**
Lime St. NN10 —1F **37**
Lime Ter. NN9 —1D **30**
Limoges Ct. NN5 —5B **6**
Linacre Clo. NN3 —1C **10**
Lincoln Rd. NN5 —4H **13**
Lincoln St. NN2 —4B **8**
Lindale Clo. NN3 —4G **9**
Linden Av. NN10 —4F **31**
Linden Ct. NN4 —4B **20**
Linden Rd. NN3 —6F **9**
Lindisfarne Way. NN4 —3B **20**
Lindsay Av. NN3 —5F **9**
Lindsay Ter. NN5 —1D **12**
Lingfield Ter. NN2 —6E **9**
Lings Way. NN3 —2D **10**
Lingswood Pk. NN3 —4D **10**
Link Rd. NN2 —1H **7**

Link Rd. NN10 —6F **37**
Links Rd. NN8 —3C **28**
Linley Grn. NN5 —1E **13**
Linnet Clo. NN8 —4A **28**
Linnetts La. NN10 —6F **31**
Lismore Clo. NN3 —5F **11**
Lister Dri. NN4 —2F **19**
Lister Rd. NN8 —6A **28**
Lit. Billing Way. NN3 —5D **10**
Littledale. NN8 —5F **27**
Lit. Gull Clo. NN3 —1C **10**
Little La. NN4 —1B **22**
Little La. NN5 —5A **24**
Lit. Park St. NN8 —6A **28**
Little St. NN10 —4G **37**
Littlewood Clo. NN5 —1H **13**
Lloyd Clo. NN8 —3B **28**
Lockcroft Sq. NN3 —5G **11**
Lockwood Clo. NN2 —3B **8**
Lodge Av. NN4 —1F **25**
Lodge Clo. NN5 —6C **6**
Lodge Clo. NN7 —6D **16**
Lodge Rd. NN7 —5D **16**
Lodge Rd. NN10 —5E **37**
Lodge Way. NN5 —4C **6**
Lodge Way. NN8 —4A **28**
Lodore Gdns. NN3 —4H **9**
Logwell Ct. NN3 —6C **10**
Lombardy Ct. NN3 —4A **10**
London End. NN6 —5B **32**
London End. NN29 —5H **35**
London Rd. NN4 —6B **14**
Longacres. NN4 —3A **20**
Longfellow Rd. NN8 —1D **32**
Longford Av. NN3 —1D **16**
Longland Ct. NN3 —5G **9**
Longland Rd. NN3 —5G **9**
Longleat Ct. NN4 —3B **20**
Long Mallows Rise. NN3 —5F **11**
Long Marsh Sq. NN3 —1D **10**
Longmead Ct. NN3 —3E **11**
Long Mynd Dri. NN5 —1E **13**
Longueville. NN3 —3B **10**
Lorne Rd. NN1 —2B **14**
Lorraine Cres. NN3 —2G **9**
Lorraine Dri. NN3 —2H **9**
Loseby Clo. NN10 —5E **37**
Louise Rd. NN1 —2C **14**
Lovat Dri. NN5 —2F **13**
Lovell Ct. NN9 —1D **30**
Lwr. Adelaide St. NN2 —2B **14**
Lwr. Cross St. NN1 —3A **14**
Lwr. Ecton La. NN3 —6G **11**
Lwr. Farm Rd. NN3 —6E **3**
Lowergrass Wlk. NN3 —6C **10**
Lwr. Harding St. NN1 —3B **14**
Lwr. Hester St. NN2 —1B **14**
Lwr. Meadow Ct. NN3 —2B **10**
Lwr. Mounts. NN1 —3C **14**
Lwr. Priory St. NN1 —2A **14**
Lower Rd. NN7 —1B **24**
Lwr. Thrift St. NN1 —3E **15**
Low Farm Pl. NN3 —6E **3**
Low Greeve. NN4 —5F **21**
Lowick Clo. NN8 —4F **27**
Lowick Ct. NN3 —6H **3**
Lowlands Clo. NN3 —2F **11**
Loxton Clo. NN5 —6D **6**
Loyd Rd. NN1 —2F **15**
Lucas Clo. NN9 —3C **30**
Ludlow Clo. NN3 —6D **4**
Lumbertubs La. NN3 —2H **9**
Lumbertubs Rise. NN3 —2A **10**
Lumbertubs Way. NN3 —1A **10**
Lutterworth Rd. NN1 —2F **15**
Lyle Ct. NN8 —4E **27**
Lyncrest Av. NN5 —2F **13**
Lyncroft Way. NN2 —6A **8**
Lyneford Way. NN10 —5D **36**
Lynmouth Av. NN3 —2H **15**
Lynton Av. NN2 —1A **8**
Lytham Clo. NN2 —4E **27**
Lytham Ct. NN8 —4E **27**
Lyttleton Rd. NN5 —2H **13**
Lyveden Rd. NN4 —2F **21**

McGibbon Wlk. NN9 —3B **30**

Maclean Clo. NN3 —2H **15**
MacMillan Way. NN3 —3G **9**
Macon Clo. NN5 —5A **6**
Magee St. NN1 —2E **15**
Maidencastle. NN3 —4E **11**
Main Rd. NN4 —6H **13**
(in two parts)
Main Rd. NN5 —5C **6**
Main Rd. NN6 & NN8 —4A **32**
Malcolm Dri. NN6 —2F **13**
Malcolm Rd. NN2 —5E **9**
Malcolm Ter. NN2 —5F **9**
Malham Ct. NN8 —5F **27**
Mallard Clo. NN4 —1G **19**
Mallard Clo. NN6 —4B **32**
Mallard Clo. NN10 —3G **31**
Mallory Clo. NN10 —2H **37**
Mallory Wlk. NN3 —2E **9**
Malpas Dri. NN5 —1C **12**
Maltings, The. NN7 —1B **24**
Malvern Gro. NN5 —1E **13**
Malzor La. NN7 —1B **24**
Manfield Rd. NN1 —2F **15**
Manfield Way. NN3 —2G **9**
Manipur. NN3 —3B **16**
Manning Ct. NN4 —6H **3**
Manning Rd. NN3 —6H **3**
Mannings Rise. NN10 —4G **37**
Mannings St. NN10 —4G **37**
Mannington Gdns. NN4 —4B **20**
Mannock Rd. NN8 —2G **33**
Manor Clo. NN9 —1F **27**
Manor Clo. NN29 —5H **35**
Manor Dri. NN3 —1E **31**
Manor Farm Rd. NN3 —5E **11**
Manorfield Clo. NN3 —1E **17**
Manorfield Rd. NN3 —1D **16**
Manor Ho. Clo. NN6 —4B **32**
Manor Rd. NN2 —4A **8**
Manor Rd. NN3 —5H **3**
Manor Rd. NN6 —4B **8**
(Earls Barton)
Manor Rd. NN6 —1C **2**
(Pitsford)
Manor Rd. NN10 —5F **37**
Manor Way. NN10 —6G **31**
Mansard Clo. NN5 —3F **13**
Mansion Clo. NN3 —1F **9**
Manton Rd. NN9 —1C **30**
Manton Rd. NN10 —4G **37**
Maple Dri. NN8 —6G **27**
Maple Rd. NN10 —3G **37**
Maple St. NN1 —2B **14**
Mapperley Dri. NN3 —1C **16**
Marble Arch. NN1 —2B **14**
Marchwood Clo. NN3 —1C **10**
Marefair. NN1 —4A **14**
Margaret Av. NN8 —3G **33**
Margaret St. NN1 —2C **14**
Marjoram Clo. NN4 —5C **20**
Market Cross. NN9 —1D **30**
Market Sq. NN1 —3B **14**
Market Sq. NN8 —1A **34**
Market Sq. NN10 —6G **31**
Market St. NN1 —2D **14**
(in two parts)
Market St. NN8 —1A **34**
Market Wlk. NN1 —2D **14**
Markham Clo. NN5 —6D **6**
Marlborough Av. NN8 —4F **27**
Marlborough Rd. NN5 —3H **13**
Marlowe Clo. NN4 —4A **20**
Marlstones. NN4 —1E **19**
Marnock Sq. NN4 —1G **19**
Marriott Clo. NN9 —3C **30**
Marriott St. NN2 —1B **14**
Marseilles Clo. NN5 —6A **6**
Marsh La. NN9 —1E **31**
Marshleys Ct. NN3 —2E **11**
Marshwell Ct. NN3 —1D **16**
Martel Clo. NN5 —1A **12**
Martindale. NN2 —2G **7**
Martins Clo. NN10 —1F **37**
Martin's La. NN4 —3C **20**
Martins Yd. NN2 —2A **14**
Marwood Clo. NN3 —2G **15**
Masefield Clo. NN8 —1E **33**
Masefield Dri. NN10 —3C **36**

Masefield Way. NN2 —5D **8**
Massey Clo. NN4 —3D **20**
Matchless Clo. NN5 —6B **6**
Mayfield Rd. NN3 —4G **9**
Mayor Hold. NN1 —3B **14**
Meadow Clo. NN5 —5C **6**
Meadow Clo. NN8 —4D **28**
Meadow Clo. NN10 —5E **31**
Meadow Dri. NN10 —5F **31**
Meadow La. NN7 —5D **16**
Meadows, The. NN9 —2G **27**
Meadow View. NN2 —1G **7**
Meadow View. NN10 —5E **31**
Meadow Wlk. NN9 —1D **30**
Meadow Wlk. NN10 —5E **31**
Meadow Way. NN9 —2D **30**
Meadway. NN3 —1A **16**
Mears Ashby Rd. NN6 —3A **32**
Mears Ashby Rd. NN8 —4D **32**
Medbourne Clo. NN3 —6G **3**
Medellin Hill. NN3 —1C **10**
Medinah Clo. NN4 —6C **20**
Medway Clo. NN5 —5F **7**
Medway Dri. NN5 —5F **7**
Medway Dri. NN8 —5E **27**
Medwin. NN8 —1D **32**
Meeting La. NN5 —2D **12**
Melbourne Ho. NN5 —3G **13**
Melbourne La. NN5 —3D **12**
Melbourne Rd. NN5 —3G **13**
Melbourne St. NN1 —3E **15**
Melbourne Wlk. NN1 —3E **15**
Melbury La. NN3 —4E **11**
Melbury Pl. NN3 —4D **10**
Melchester Clo. NN4 —4D **20**
Meldon Clo. NN4 —4B **20**
Melloway Rd. NN10 —3C **36**
Melrose Av. NN5 —2F **13**
Meltham Clo. NN3 —6C **10**
Melton Rd. NN8 —6C **28**
Melton Rd. N. NN8 —6B **28**
Melville St. NN1 —2E **15**
Memorial Sq. NN1 —3B **14**
Mendip Rd. NN5 —1E **13**
Meon Way. NN5 —1E **13**
Mercers Row. NN1 —4B **14**
Mercia Gdns. NN3 —6H **9**
Mercury Dri. NN4 —1F **21**
Mere Clo. NN4 —3A **20**
Mere Clo. NN7 —1G **23**
Mere Way. NN4 —2H **19**
Merlin Gro. NN4 —3A **20**
Merrydale Sq. NN3 —1D **10**
Merryhill. NN4 —1F **19**
Mershe Clo. NN4 —4E **21**
Merthyr Rd. NN5 —1H **13**
Meshaw Cres. NN3 —2G **15**
Mews, The. NN3 —1A **16**
Micklewell La. NN3 —1C **10**
Middle Greeve. NN4 —5F **21**
Middlemarch. NN3 —3E **11**
Middle Mead Ct. NN8 —6D **10**
Middlemore. NN3 —1C **10**
Middleton Clo. NN2 —2B **8**
Middlewell Ct. NN3 —6C **10**
Midfield Ct. NN3 —2B **10**
Midland Rd. NN8 —1A **34**
Midland Rd. NN10 —5G **31**
(Higham Ferrers)
Midland Rd. NN10 —2E **37**
(Rushden)
Milbury. NN6 —6C **32**
Miles Well Ct. NN3 —4A **10**
Military Rd. NN1 —2C **14**
Millbank. NN3 —5G **11**
Millbrook Clo. NN5 —5H **13**
Millerhill. NN4 —1F **19**
Millers La. NN8 —5H **33**
Millers Pk. NN8 —4A **34**
Mill Est. NN10 —6F **37**
Mill La. NN2 —2A **14**
(Northampton)
Mill La. NN5 & NN2 —1G **13**
(Dallington & Kingsthorpe)
Mill Meadow. NN2 —2C **8**
Mill Rd. NN2 —2B **14**
Mill Rd. NN8 —6B **28**
(in two parts)

Mill Rd. Ind. Est. NN8 —5D **28**
Mills Clo. NN6 —5C **32**
Millside Clo. NN2 —2C **8**
Millway. NN5 —3D **12**
Milton Av. NN8 —2E **33**
Milton Ct. NN7 —2B **24**
Milton Rd. NN8 —4C **34**
Milton St. NN2 —6D **8**
Milton St. NN10 —6F **31**
Milton St. N. NN2 —5D **8**
Milverton Cres. NN3 —2H **15**
Minverva Way. NN8 —6F **27**
Mitchell Clo. NN5 —5E **7**
Moat Pl. NN1 —3A **14**
Moffatt Ter. NN8 —6A **28**
Monarch Rd. NN2 —6B **8**
Monarch Ter. NN2 —1B **14**
Monks Hall Rd. NN1 —2E **15**
Monks Pk. Rd. NN1 —2E **15**
Monks Pond St. NN1 —3A **14**
Monks Way. NN8 —2A **34**
Monmouth Rd. NN5 —2H **13**
Montague Cres. NN5 —5E **7**
Montague St. NN10 —3E **37**
Montfort Clo. NN5 —3F **13**
Moore St. NN2 —6E **9**
Moorfield Sq. NN3 —1D **10**
Moorland Clo. NN5 —5B **10**
Moorlands. NN8 —4E **27**
Moor Rd. NN10 —2E **37**
Moray Lodge. NN5 —2C **12**
Mordaunt La. NN5 —6E **7**
Moreton Way. NN2 —2B **8**
Morgan Clo. NN3 —3F **11**
Morris Av. NN10 —4D **36**
Morris Clo. NN8 —5C **26**
Morris Rd. NN2 —4C **8**
Mortar Pit Rd. NN3 —2F **11**
Motspur Dri. NN2 —6A **8**
Moulton La. NN2 —5B **2**
Moulton Rd. NN6 —1C **2**
Moulton Way. NN3 —1G **9**
Moulton Way N. NN3 —1H **9**
Moulton Way S. NN3 —1H **9**
Mountclaire Ct. NN3 —1B **16**
Mountfield Rd. NN3 —4F **9**
Mt. Pleasant. NN6 —6C **32**
Mounts Clo. NN3 —4B **10**
Muirfield Rd. NN8 —4E **27**
Mulberry Clo. NN5 —2G **13**
Mumford Dri. NN7 —4B **18**
Muncaster Gdns. NN4 —4C **20**
Murray Av. NN2 —6C **8**
Muscott La. NN5 —3C **12**
Muscott St. NN5 —2H **13**
Mushroom Field Rd. NN3 —5G **11**

Naomi Clo. NN3 —6C **10**
Napier Clo. NN8 —1C **32**
Narrow La. NN1 —3B **14**
Naseby Clo. NN8 —4F **27**
Naseby St. NN2 —1B **14**
Navigation Row. NN1 —5B **14**
Neale Clo. NN3 —1A **16**
Neilson Rd. NN8 —3C **28**
Nelson St. NN2 —2B **14**
Nene Clo. NN8 —5E **27**
Nene Ct. NN8 —2C **34**
Nene Dri. NN5 —5E **7**
Nene Rise. NN7 —3H **17**
Nene Rd. NN10 —6F **31**
Nene Valley Way. NN4 & NN3 —2C **20**
Nene View. NN9 —1D **30**
Nene Wlk. NN5 —5G **7**
Nene Way. NN5 —5G **7**
Nesbitt Clo. NN3 —2B **16**
Nest Farm Cres. NN8 —3A **28**
Nest Farm Rd. NN8 —4A **28**
Nest Farm Way. NN8 —4A **28**
Nest La. NN8 —5B **28**
Nether Jackson Ct. NN3 —3E **11**
Nether Mead Ct. NN3 —3C **10**
Newbury Clo. NN10 —2H **37**
Newby Ct. NN3 —4H **9**
Newcombe Rd. NN5 —2H **13**
Newcomen Rd. NN8 —6B **28**
Newington Rd. NN2 —3B **8**

Newland. NN1 —3B **14**
Newland Sq. NN2 —3B **8**
Newland Wlk. NN1 —3C **14**
(off Peacock Pl.)
Newman St. NN10 —4G **31**
Newnham Rd. NN2 —4C **8**
Newport Pagnell Rd. NN4 —3C **20**
Newport Rd. NN5 —2H **13**
New Rd. NN4 —5D **20**
Newstead Clo. NN3 —4G **11**
Newstone Cres. NN4 —5F **13**
New St. NN6 —5C **32**
New St. NN8 —6A **28**
New St. NN9 —1D **30**
New St. NN29 —5H **35**
Newton Clo. NN8 —5D **26**
Newton Clo. NN10 —4H **37**
Newton Rd. NN5 —6D **6**
Newton Rd. NN10 —5H **31**
(Higham Ferrers)
Newton Rd. NN10 —3F **37**
(Rushden)
Newtown Rd. NN1 —3E **15**
Newtown Rd. NN8 —4C **34**
Nicholas Rd. NN9 —2C **30**
Nicholas Way. NN10 —2D **36**
Nicholls Clo. NN3 —2B **10**
Nightingale La. NN8 —4B **28**
Niort Way. NN8 —5D **26**
Nippendale. NN10 —3G **37**
Norfolk St. NN2 —1B **14**
Norman D Gate. NN1 —4D **14**
Norman D Gate Ind. Est. NN1 —4D **14**
Norman Rd. NN3 —6G **9**
Norman Way. NN8 —3F **33**
Norman Way. NN29 —5A **36**
Normead Sq. NN3 —5G **11**
Norris Way. NN10 —2C **36**
Norris Way Ind. Est. NN10 —2C **36**
Northampton Airport. (Sywell) NN6 —1H **5**
Northampton La. N. NN3 —5H **3**
Northampton La. S. NN3 —1G **9**
Northampton Rd. NN6 —4A **32**
Northampton Rd. NN7 —4A **24**
(Blisworth)
Northampton Rd. NN7 —6F **25**
(Courteenhall)
Northampton Rd. NN8 —3E **33**
Northampton Rd. NN10 —2A **34**
Northcote St. NN2 —2B **14**
North End. NN10 —5F **31**
Northen Rd. NN8 —3G **27**
Northfield Rd. NN5 —6C **6**
Northfield Way. NN2 —3A **8**
N. Heyes Ct. NN3 —2C **10**
N. Holme Ct. NN3 —2A **10**
N. Leys Ct. NN3 —6H **3**
N. Oval. NN5 —5G **7**
N. Paddock Ct. NN3 —3C **10**
N. Portway Clo. NN3 —6C **4**
N. Priors Ct. NN3 —3D **10**
North Rd. NN6 —4B **32**
North St. NN7 —5B **18**
North St. NN8 —6H **27**
North St. NN10 —2F **37**
Northumbria Gdns. NN3 —6G **9**
N. Western Av. NN2 —3H **7**
Northwood Rd. NN3 —5G **9**
Norton Rd. NN2 —4B **8**
Notre Dame M. NN1 —3C **14**
Nunn Mills Rd. NN1 —5D **14**
Nurseries, The. NN3 —4H **3**
Nursery Dri. NN8 —4B **28**
Nursery Gdns. NN8 —1C **30**
Nursery La. NN2 —4B **8**
Nuthall Clo. NN3 —1C **16**

Oakgrove Pl. NN4 —5C **20**
Oakham Clo. NN3 —1G **9**
Oakham Clo. NN10 —5E **37**
Oakham Clo. NN10 —6A **10**
Oaklands Dri. NN3 —6A **10**
Oakleigh Dri. NN5 —6D **6**
Oakley Dri. NN3 —4A **4**
Oakley Dri. NN8 —1F **33**
Oakley Rd. NN10 —2D **36**
Oakley St. NN1 —2C **14**

Oakmont Clo. NN4 —6B **20**
Oakpark Clo. NN3 —1D **10**
Oakpits Way. NN10 —4G **37**
Oaks Dri. NN10 —4F **31**
Oak St. NN1 —2B **14**
Oak St. NN10 —1F **37**
Oak St. NN29 —6G **35**
Oak Ter. NN9 —1D **30**
Oakway. NN8 —4H **27**
Oak Way. NN9 —1D **30**
(Irthlingborough)
Oak Way. NN9 —2H **27**
(Wellingborough)
Oakwood Rd. NN1 —6E **9**
Oat Hill Dri. NN3 —5G **11**
Obelisk Clo. NN2 —5B **2**
Obelisk Ho. NN2 —6B **2**
Obelisk Rise. NN2 —6B **2**
Old Barn Ct. NN3 —4C **10**
Old Bedford Rd. NN4 —5G **15**
Oldenmead Ct. NN3 —4C **10**
Olden Rd. NN3 —2F **11**
Old Quarry Ct. NN3 —3B **10**
Old Towcester Rd. NN4 —5B **14**
Old Vineyard, The. NN10 —5F **31**
Old Yew Ct. NN2 —4A **8**
Oleander Cres. NN3 —3F **11**
Oliver Clo. NN3 —3G **37**
Oliver St. NN2 —6D **8**
Olympia Clo. NN4 —3A **20**
Olympic Way. NN8 —6E **27**
Oransay Clo. NN3 —5F **11**
Orchard Clo. NN4 —5D **20**
Orchard Clo. NN7 —1B **24**
Orchard Cotts. NN7 —4D **16**
Orchard Grn. NN3 —5H **9**
Orchard Hill. NN3 —6D **10**
Orchard Ho. NN8 —5A **28**
Orchard Pl. NN29 —5G **35**
Orchard St. NN5 —3H **13**
Orchard Ter. NN8 —1H **33**
Orchard Way. NN5 —3D **12**
Orchard Way. NN7 —3H **17**
Orient Way. NN8 —1A **34**
Orlingbury Rd. NN9 —1F **27**
Orton Pl. NN8 —4F **27**
Orwell Clo. NN8 —5E **27**
Osborn Ct. NN8 —2G **33**
Osborne Clo. NN10 —1H **37**
Osborne Rd. NN2 —5B **8**
Osler Clo. NN2 —2A **8**
Osmund Dri. NN3 —2D **10**
Osprey La. NN8 —4B **28**
Osprey Rise. NN4 —3A **20**
Osprey View. NN4 —3A **20**
Oswald Rd. NN10 —3G **37**
Osyth Clo. NN4 —1F **21**
Oulton Rise. NN10 —2F **37**
Oundle Dri. NN3 —6G **3**
Ouse Clo. NN8 —5E **27**
Outlaw La. NN8 —6H **27**
Oval Cres. NN10 —3H **37**
Oval Rd. NN10 —3H **37**
Overleys Ct. NN3 —2E **11**
Overmead Rd. NN8 —5F **11**
Overslade Clo. NN4 —3H **19**
Overstone Cres. NN6 —4E **5**
Overstone La. NN3 —4B **4**
(Moulton)
Overstone La. NN3 —2E **11**
(Rectory Farm, in two parts)
Overstone Rd. NN1 —3C **14**
Overstone Rd. NN3 —4A **4**
Overstone Rd. NN6 —3F **5**
Owen Clo. NN8 —6D **26**
Owen M. NN8 —6D **26**
Owl Clo. NN3 —6E **3**
Oxburgh Ct. NN4 —3B **20**
Oxford Clo. NN6 —6C **32**
Oxford Ho. NN8 —1H **33**
Oxford St. NN4 —6A **14**
Oxford St. NN8 —1H **33**
Oxford St. NN10 —6E **37**
Oxwich Clo. NN4 —2F **21**

Paddock Mill Ct. NN3 —3E **11**
Paddocks Rd. NN10 —2C **36**

Paddocks Way. NN3 —6D **10**
Padwell Ct. NN3 —1D **16**
Paget Clo. NN4 —1B **22**
Palk Rd. NN8 —1B **34**
Palmer Clo. NN8 —4F **27**
Palmer Sq. NN3 —6F **11**
Palmerston Ct. NN1 —3D **14**
Palmerston Rd. NN1 —3D **14**
Palm Rd. NN10 —2C **36**
Parade Bank. NN3 —4H **3**
Parade, The. NN1 —3B **14**
Park Av. NN1 —1F **15**
Park Av. NN5 —6B **6**
Park Av. NN10 —4D **36**
Park Av. N. NN3 —5F **9**
Park Av. S. NN3 —1F **15**
Park Clo. NN6 —3F **5**
Park Clo. NN7 —1H **23**
Park Cres. E. NN5 —5G **7**
Park Cres. W. NN5 —6G **7**
Park Dri. NN5 —6G **7**
Park Farm Ind. Est. NN8 —5D **26**
Park Farm Way. NN8 —2C **32**
Parkfield Av. NN4 —1B **20**
Parkfield Cres. NN4 —1B **20**
Park Gro. NN8 —6A **28**
Park Hill Rd. NN3 —4A **10**
Parklands. NN6 —4G **5**
Parklands Av. NN3 —2F **9**
Parklands Cres. NN3 —2F **9**
Park La. NN5 —6B **6**
Park La. NN6 —5A **32**
Park Pl. NN3 —3F **37**
Park Rd. NN8 —6A **28**
Park Rd. NN9 —2C **30**
Park Rd. NN10 —3F **37**
Parkside. NN3 —5G **11**
Park Sq. NN5 —5G **7**
Park St. NN6 —5A **32**
Park View. NN3 —4B **4**
Park View Clo. NN3 —4B **4**
Park Wlk. NN5 —6G **7**
Parkway. NN3 —1A **16**
Parkwood St. NN5 —3A **14**
Parracombe Way. NN3 —2H **15**
Parsons Mead. NN4 —1F **19**
Parsons Rd. NN29 —5H **35**
Partridge Clo. NN2 —2H **7**
Parva Ct. NN3 —4B **10**
Pasteur Clo. NN2 —2A **8**
Pastures, The. NN2 —2H **7**
Pastures, The. NN9 —2G **27**
Paterson Rd. NN8 —3B **28**
Patterdale Wlk. NN3 —3H **9**
Patterson Clo. NN3 —6B **10**
Paxton Rd. NN3 —6B **10**
Peace Clo. NN4 —6G **13**
Peacock Pl. NN1 —3C **14**
Peacock Way. NN1 —3C **14**
Pearmain Av. NN8 —4H **27**
Pearmain Ct. NN3 —5D **10**
Pear Tree Clo. NN3 —5D **10**
Pebble La. NN8 —1A **34**
Pelham St. NN3 —3A **10**
Pell Ct. NN3 —4B **10**
Pemberton Rd. NN10 —3E **37**
Pembroke Clo. NN10 —4G **37**
Pembroke Cres. NN5 —1H **13**
Pembroke Gdns. NN5 —1H **13**
Pembroke Rd. NN5 —1H **13**
Penarth Rd. NN5 —1H **13**
Pendered Rd. NN4 —4A **34**
Pendle Rd. NN5 —1D **12**
Penfold Clo. NN2 —3A **8**
Penfold Dri. NN3 —4E **11**
Penfold Gdns. NN3 —4F **11**
Penfold La. NN3 —4F **11**
Penistone Rd. NN3 —4B **10**
Penistone Wlk. NN3 —4B **10**
Pennard Clo. NN4 —1G **21**
Penn Gdns. NN4 —2A **20**
Pennine Way. NN5 —2E **13**
Pennycress Pl. NN3 —6F **11**
Penrhyn Rd. NN4 —6B **14**
Penvale Rd. NN4 —5A **20**
Peppercorn Way. NN4 —5C **20**
Perceval Clo. NN5 —6E **7**
Percy Rd. NN1 —2E **15**

Peregrine Pl. NN4 —3H **19**
Perkins Ct. NN8 —6A **28**
Perkins Rd. NN9 —3C **30**
Perry St. NN1 —2E **15**
Pevensey Clo. NN10 —4H **37**
Peverel Clo. NN10 —5G **31**
Peverel's Way. NN5 —3F **13**
Peveril Rd. NN5 —2D **12**
Pheasant Way. NN2 —2H **7**
Philip Way. NN10 —4G **31**
Phippsville Ct. NN1 —6E **9**
Phoenix St. NN1 —3B **14**
Piccadilly Clo. NN4 —1G **19**
Pie Corner. NN6 —2G **5**
Pightles Ter. NN10 —4G **37**
Pike La. NN1 —3B **14**
Pikemead Ct. NN3 —3E **11**
Pilgrims Pl. NN4 —1B **20**
Pilgrim Way. NN8 —2H **33**
Pilton Clo. NN3 —2F **11**
Pindar Rise. NN3 —1B **10**
Pindar Rd. NN8 —3G **33**
Pine Av. NN6 —4G **5**
Pine Clo. NN10 —5E **37**
Pine Clo. NN29 —6G **35**
Pine Copse Clo. NN5 —5B **6**
Pine Cres. NN6 —4G **5**
Pineham Av. NN2 —1C **8**
Pine Ridge. NN3 —6C **4**
Pine Trees. NN3 —6A **10**
Pinewood Rd. NN3 —4G **9**
Pippin Clo. NN7 —4H **17**
Pippin Clo. NN10 —2C **36**
Pippin La. NN3 —5D **10**
Pitsford Rd. NN3 —3E **3**
Pitstone Rd. NN4 —6F **13**
Pitt St. NN8 —1G **33**
Plantagenet Sq. NN4 —1G **19**
Pleydell Rd. NN4 —1B **20**
Plough La. NN2 —1H **7**
Ploughmans Wlk. NN2 —2A **8**
Plumtree Av. NN8 —4A **28**
Poachers Way. NN2 —2A **8**
Poitiers Ct. NN5 —6A **6**
Pond Bank. NN7 —5A **24**
Pond Farm Clo. NN5 —2D **12**
Pond Wood Clo. NN3 —1G **9**
Poole St. NN1 —2C **14**
Pope Rd. NN8 —2E **33**
Poplar Clo. NN10 —5E **37**
Poplar Clo. NN29 —6G **35**
Poplar Ct. NN3 —2A **10**
Poplar St. NN8 —6A **28**
Poppy Clo. NN10 —5G **37**
Poppyfield Ct. NN3 —3C **10**
Porlock Clo. NN5 —1F **13**
Portchester Gdns. NN3 —1B **16**
Portland Pl. NN1 —2D **14**
Portland Rd. NN9 —1D **30**
Portland Rd. NN10 —3F **37**
Port Rd. NN5 —5B **6**
Portstone Clo. NN5 —5B **6**
Pound La. NN3 —5F **11**
(Great Billing)
Pound La. NN3 —4G **3**
(Moulton)
Poyntz Gdns. NN5 —1F **13**
Poyntz La. NN5 —1F **13**
Pratt Rd. NN10 —3G **37**
Premier Way. NN9 —3C **30**
Prentice Ct. NN3 —2D **10**
Prescott Clo. NN3 —3F **11**
Pressland Dri. NN10 —5G **31**
Prestbury Rd. NN5 —6B **6**
Preston Ct. NN3 —4B **10**
Prestwold Way. NN3 —2E **11**
Primrose Hill. NN2 —1B 14
(off Kingsthorpe Rd.)
Prince of Wales Row. NN3 —4A **4**
Princess Clo. NN3 —3G **15**
Princess Wlk. NN1 —3C 14
(off Peacock Pl.)
Princess Way. NN8 —3G **33**
Prince St. NN8 —4B **32**
Priors Clo. NN10 —5D **36**
Priory Clo. NN3 —3G **15**
Priory Rd. NN8 —3H **33**
Priory, The. NN3 —3H **15**

Pritchard Clo. NN3 —1F **11**
Promenade, The. NN8 —6G **27**
Prospect Av. NN10 —1F **37**
Prospect Av. NN29 —6F **35**
Provence Ct. NN5 —6A **6**
Purbeck Rd. NN10 —3B **36**
Purser Rd. NN1 —1E **15**
Purvis Rd. NN10 —3E **37**
Pyghtle, The. NN6 —4B **32**
Pyghtle, The. NN8 —5A **28**
Pyghtle Way. NN4 —4H **19**
Pyket Way. NN3 —1B **16**
Pytchley Rise. NN8 —2F **33**
Pytchley Rd. NN10 —2D **36**
Pytchley St. NN1 —3D **14**
Pytchley View. NN3 —4A **4**
Pytchley Way. NN5 —5C **6**

Quantock Cres. NN5 —1E **13**
Quarry Pk. Clo. NN3 —1G **9**
Quarry Rd. NN5 —5C **6**
Quartercraft. NN3 —5B **10**
Quebec Rd. NN4 —4D **20**
Queen Eleanor Rd. NN4 —1A **20**
Queen Eleanor Ter. NN4 —1B **20**
Queens Cres. NN2 —5C **8**
Queensland Gdns. NN2 —5B **8**
Queens Pk. Pde. NN2 —5B **8**
Queens Rd. NN1 —2D **14**
Queen St. NN6 —4B **32**
Queen St. NN8 —6A **28**
Queen St. NN9 —1C **30**
Queen St. NN10 —3F **37**
Queensway. NN8 —1E **33**
Queensway. NN10 —6G **31**
Queenswood Av. NN3 —3H **9**
Quernstone La. NN6 —4F **13**
Quinton Rd. NN4 —6D **20**
Quorn Clo. NN8 —1F **33**
Quorn Rd. NN10 —2D **36**
Quorn Way. NN1 —2A **14**

Racedown. NN8 —2D **32**
Radstone Way. NN2 —2B **8**
Raeburn Rd. NN2 —5D **8**
Raglan Clo. NN10 —4H **37**
Raglan St. NN1 —3D **14**
Ragsdale Wlk. NN3 —1A **10**
Rainsborough Cres. NN4 —5G **13**
Raisins Field Clo. NN3 —4F **11**
Rakestone Clo. NN4 —5C **20**
Randall Rd. NN2 —6D **8**
Ranelagh Rd. NN8 —6B **28**
Ransome Rd. NN4 —6C **14**
Ravensbank. NN10 —1F **37**
Ravens Croft. NN4 —4H **19**
Ravens Way. NN3 —1F **17**
Rawley Cres. NN5 —6B **6**
Raymond Rd. NN5 —2H **13**
Raynsford Rd. NN5 —6G **7**
Rea Clo. NN4 —4B **20**
Rectory Clo. NN4 —1B **22**
Rectory Clo. NN10 —3F **37**
Rectory Farm Rd. NN3 —2F **11**
Rectory La. NN7 —2B **24**
Rectory Rd. NN10 —2F **37**
Redhill Way. NN9 —3G **27**
Redhouse Rd. NN4 —6E **3**
Redland Dri. NN2 —3H **7**
Redruth Clo. NN4 —2A **20**
Redwell Rd. NN8 —5H **27**
Redwing Av. NN3 —1H **9**
Redwood Clo. NN29 —6G **35**
Reedham Clo. NN5 —6D **6**
Reedhill. NN4 —2F **9**
Reedway. NN3 —3F **9**
Regal Ct. NN10 —4G **37**
Regent Sq. NN1 —2B **14**
Regent St. NN1 —3B **14**
Reims Ct. NN5 —5B **6**
Rennishaw Way. NN2 —4E **9**
Repton Clo. NN3 —3A **10**
Resthaven Rd. NN4 —5D **20**
Restormel Clo. NN10 —4H **37**
Retford Ct. NN3 —3C **10**

Reynard Way. NN2 —1C **8**
Reynolds Clo. NN9 —3C **30**
Rhosili Rd. NN4 —1E **21**
Ribble Clo. NN5 —5G **7**
Richmond Clo. NN10 —4G **37**
Richmond Ter. NN5 —3A **14**
Rickyard Rd. NN3 —4A **10**
Rides Ct. NN3 —6H **3**
Ridge, The. NN29 —5H **33**
Ridgewalk. NN3 —4G **11**
　(Great Billing)
Ridge Wlk. NN3 —1B **16**
　(Weston Favell)
Ridgeway. NN3 —1H **15**
Ridgeway. NN8 —4H **27**
Ridings, The. NN1 —3C **14**
Riley Clo. NN3 —2F **11**
Rillwood Ct. NN3 —3B **10**
Ring Way. NN4 —6H **13**
Ringwood Clo. NN2 —2H **7**
Rise, The. NN2 —4B **8**
Riverside Way. NN1 —4E **15**
Riverwell. NN3 —5G **11**
Rixon Clo. NN3 —6B **10**
Rixon Rd. NN3 —3B **28**
Roberts St. NN8 —1G **33**
Roberts St. NN10 —3G **37**
Robert St. NN1 —2C **14**
Robinia Clo. NN4 —6F **13**
Robin La. NN8 —4A **28**
Robinson Rd. NN10 —3G **37**
Rochelle Way. NN5 —5B **6**
Roche Way. NN8 —5H **27**
Rockcroft Clo. NN4 —5C **20**
Rockingham Ct. NN10 —5E **37**
Rockingham Rd. NN4 —1B **20**
Rock St. NN8 —6H **27**
Roe Rd. NN1 —1E **15**
Rokeby Wlk. NN5 —6E **7**
Roland Way. NN10 —5F **31**
Roman Way. NN29 —6H **35**
Romany Rd. NN2 —6D **8**
Rookery La. NN2 —1H **7**
Rose Av. NN10 —4D **36**
Roseberry Av. NN5 —3G **13**
Rosedale Rd. NN2 —4C **8**
Roseholme Rd. NN1 —2F **15**
Rosemoor Dri. NN4 —4B **20**
Rosenella Clo. NN4 —6G **13**
Rose Villa. NN1 —4E **15**
Rosgill Pl. NN3 —5G **9**
Rossette Clo. NN5 —1D **12**
Ross Rd. NN5 —3F **13**
Rothersthorpe Av. NN4 —6H **13**
Rothersthorpe Cres. NN4 —6H **13**
Rothersthorpe La. NN4 —1H **19**
Rothersthorpe Rd. NN4 —1G **19**
Rothersthorpe Rd. NN7 —3A **18**
Rothesay Rd. NN2 —5E **9**
Rothesay Ter. NN2 —5E **9**
Rowan Av. NN3 —2H **9**
Rowan Clo. NN8 —6G **27**
Rowlandson Clo. NN3 —6B **10**
Rowlett Clo. NN10 —6G **31**
Rowtree Rd. NN4 —4G **19**
Royal Ter. NN1 —2B **14**
Rubble Clo. NN8 —5F **27**
Rudge M. NN5 —1A **12**
Runnymede Gdns. NN3 —6C **10**
Rushden Rd. NN10 —6E **37**
Rushmere Av. NN1 —3G **15**
Rushmere Cres. NN1 —3G **15**
Rushmere Rd. NN1 —5F **15**
Rushmere Way. NN10 —1E **37**
Rushmills. NN4 —6G **15**
Rushy End. NN4 —5A **20**
Ruskin Av. NN8 —1E **33**
Ruskin Rd. NN2 —3B **8**
Russell Ct. NN10 —3F **37**
Russell Sq. NN3 —1H **9**
Russell Ter. NN1 —4C **14**
Russell Way. NN10 —5F **31**
Russett Dri. NN3 —5D **10**
Rutherford Dri. NN8 —1C **32**
Rutland Wlk. NN3 —6G **3**
Rydal. NN8 —2D **32**
Rydal Mt. NN3 —4H **9**
Rydalside. NN4 —6G **13**

Ryder View. NN8 —4E **27**
Ryebury Hill. NN9 —1E **29**
Ryehill Clo. NN5 —5D **6**
Ryehill Ct. NN5 —5D **6**
Ryehill Rd. NN3 —4C **10**
Ryeland Rd. NN5 —1B **12**
Ryeland Way. NN5 —6B **6**
Ryland Rd. NN2 —5D **8**
Ryland Rd. NN3 —5H **3**
Rylstone, The. NN8 —2D **32**

Saddleback Rd. NN5 —3E **13**
Saddlers Sq. NN3 —1C **10**
Saffron Clo. NN4 —6C **20**
Saffron Rd. NN10 —4F **31**
Sage Clo. NN3 —3B **10**
St Alban's Clo. NN3 —4G **9**
St Alban's Rd. NN3 —4G **9**
St Andrews Cres. NN8 —4G **33**
St Andrew's Rd. NN1 & NN2 —3A **14**
St Andrew's St. NN1 —3B **14**
St Barnabas St. NN8 —1G **33**
St Benedict's Mt. NN4 —2F **19**
St Catherine's Ct. NN1 —3B 14
　(off Phoenix St.)
St Christopher's Wlk. NN3 —2G **15**
St Crispin Av. NN8 —3H **33**
St Crispin Rd. NN6 —5C **32**
St David's Rd. NN2 —5B **8**
St Dunstans Rise. NN4 —2F **19**
St Edmund's Rd. NN1 —3D **14**
St Edmund's St. NN1 —3D **14**
St Edmund's Ter. NN1 —3D **14**
St Emilion Clo. NN5 —6A **6**
St Francis Av. NN5 —1H **13**
St George's Av. NN2 —1B **14**
St Georges Pl. NN2 —1B 14
　(off Kingsthorpe Rd.)
St Georges St. NN1 —2B **14**
St George's Way. NN10 —2D **36**
St Giles Sq. NN1 —4C **14**
St Giles St. NN1 —4C **14**
St Giles Ter. NN1 —3C **14**
St Gregory's Rd. NN3 —4A **10**
St James' Clo. NN10 —1F **37**
St James' Mill Rd. NN5 —4A **14**
St James' Mill Rd. E. NN1 —5A **14**
St James' Pk. Rd. NN5 —3H **13**
St James Pl. NN1 —4B **14**
St James' Rd. NN5 & NN1 —3H **13**
St James St. NN1 —4B **14**
St John's Av. NN2 —1B **8**
St John's St. NN1 —4B **14**
St John's St. NN8 —6H **27**
St Johns Ter. NN1 —4C **14**
St Julien Clo. NN5 —5B **6**
St Katherine's Sq. NN1 —3B **14**
St Katherine's St. NN1 —4B **14**
St Katherine's Way. NN29 —4H **35**
St Leonard's Rd. NN4 —6B **14**
St Margaret's Gdns. NN5 —6G **7**
St Margarets Rd. NN10 —4D **36**
St Mark's Clo. NN10 —3C **36**
St Marks Cres. NN2 —1A **8**
St Martins Clo. NN2 —3B **8**
St Mary's Av. NN10 —4E **37**
St Mary's Ct. NN1 —3B 14
　(off Horsemarket)
St Mary's St. NN1 —3B **14**
St Matthew's Pde. NN1 —6E **9**
St Michael's Av. NN1 —2D **14**
St Michael's Mt. NN1 —2D **14**
St Michael's Rd. NN1 —3C **14**
St Patrick St. NN1 —2B **14**
St Pauls Rd. NN2 —1B **14**
St Paul's Ter. NN2 —1B **14**
St Peter's Av. NN10 —2D **36**
St Peter's Gdns. NN3 —6A **14**
St Peter's Sq. NN1 —4A **14**
St Peter's Way. NN1 —4A **14**
St Peters Way. NN7 —3H **17**
St Peter's Way. NN9 —1D **30**
Salcey St. NN4 —1B **20**
Salem La. NN8 —6H **27**
Salisbury Rd. NN8 —6C **28**
Salisbury St. NN2 —1B **14**
Sallow Av. NN3 —4F **11**

Salthouse Rd. NN4 —1F **21**
Saltwell Sq. NN3 —5F **11**
Sanders Clo. NN8 —3B **28**
Sanders Lodge Ind. Est. NN10
　　　　　　　　　—2B **36**
Sanders Rd. NN8 —2A **28**
Sandfield Clo. NN3 —1G **9**
Sandhill Rd. NN5 —3H **13**
Sandhills Clo. NN2 —1A **8**
Sandhills Rd. NN2 —1A **8**
Sandiland Rd. NN3 —5G **9**
Sandover. NN4 —5C **20**
Sandpiper La. NN8 —4A **28**
Sandringham Clo. NN1 —2G **15**
Sandringham Clo. NN10 —4E **37**
Sandringham Rd. NN1 —2F **15**
Sandy Clo. NN8 —5H **27**
Sandy La. NN7 & NN5 —2A **12**
Sansom Clo. NN3 —1G **9**
Sarek Pk. NN4 —4G **19**
Sargeants La. NN4 —1F **25**
Sartoris Rd. NN10 —3D **36**
Saruman La. NN3 —1E **11**
Sassoon Clo. NN8 —5D **26**
Sassoon Ct. NN8 —6D **26**
Savill Clo. NN4 —4B **20**
Saxby Clo. NN8 —1C **34**
Saxon Rise. NN5 —2C **12**
Saxon Rise. NN6 —5B **32**
Saxon Rise. NN29 —5A **36**
Saxon St. NN3 —6G **9**
Scarborough St. NN9 —1C **30**
Scarletwell St. NN1 —3A **14**
Scarletwell Ter. NN1 —3A **14**
Scarplands, The. NN5 —3D **12**
School Hill. NN29 —5H **35**
School La. NN3 —4H **3**
School La. NN29 —5G **35**
School Rd. NN29 —5G **35**
School Way. NN3 —5H **9**
Scirocco Clo. NN2 —1D **8**
Scotia Clo. NN4 —1H **21**
Scotney Clo. NN4 —3B **20**
Scott Rd. NN8 —2E **33**
Seagrave Ct. NN3 —2E **11**
Seaton Dri. NN3 —6C **10**
Second Av. NN8 —2E **33**
Sedgwick Ct. NN3 —4C **10**
Seedfield Clo. NN3 —6B **10**
Seedfield Wlk. NN3 —1C **16**
Selston Wlk. NN3 —2A **16**
Semilong Pl. NN2 —2B **14**
Semilong Rd. NN2 —2B **14**
Sentinel Rd. NN4 —2F **19**
Senwick Dri. NN8 —1C **34**
Senwick Rd. NN8 —1C **34**
Severn Clo. NN8 —5E **27**
Severn Dri. NN5 —5G **7**
Seymour St. NN5 —3H **13**
Shadowfax Dri. NN3 —2E **11**
Shakespeare Rd. NN1 —2D **14**
Shakespeare Rd. NN8 —2D **32**
Shakespeare Rd. NN10 —3C **36**
Shannon Clo. NN10 —2H **37**
Shap Grn. NN3 —3H **9**
Shard Clo. NN4 —5B **20**
Sharman Rd. NN5 —4H **13**
Sharman Rd. NN8 —1H **33**
Sharrow Pl. NN3 —5G **11**
Sharwood Ter. NN29 —5G **35**
Shatterstone. NN4 —5C **20**
Shaw Clo. NN8 —6D **26**
Sheaf Clo. NN5 —5C **6**
Shearwater La. NN8 —4A **28**
Shedfield Way. NN4 —5B **20**
Sheep St. NN1 —3B **14**
Sheep St. NN8 —1A **34**
Sheerwater Dri. NN3 —4G **11**
Sheffield Way. NN6 —6B **32**
Shelford Clo. NN3 —2E **11**
Shelley Dri. NN10 —6E **31**
Shelley Rd. NN8 —1D **32**
Shelley St. NN2 —6E **9**
Shelsley Dri. NN3 —3E **9**
Shepherd Clo. NN2 —2H **7**
Shepperton Clo. NN3 —5F **11**
Sheraton Clo. NN3 —5H **9**
Sheriff Rd. NN1 —2E **15**

Sherwood Av. NN2 —1G **7**
Shipton Way. NN10 —2A **36**
Shire Pl. NN3 —2E **11**
Shirley Rd. NN10 —2F **37**
Shoal Creek. NN4 —6B **20**
Short La. NN8 —6H **27**
Short Stocks. NN10 —2H **37**
Shurville Clo. NN6 —6C **32**
Siddons Way. NN3 —4A **4**
Sidebrook Ct. NN3 —2C **10**
Sidegate La. NN8 —2E **29**
Sidings, The. NN9 —3B **30**
Silverdale Gro. NN10 —3C **36**
Silverdale Rd. NN3 —5A **10**
Silverstone Clo. NN2 —2C **8**
Silver St. NN1 —3B **14**
Silver St. NN8 —1A **34**
Simon's Wlk. NN1 —3B **14**
Simpson Rd. NN4 —4G **31**
Sinclair Dri. NN8 —5C **26**
Sir John Pascoe Way. NN5 —1D **12**
Siward View. NN5 —5E **7**
Six Acre Wlk. NN3 —5F **11**
Skawle Ct. NN3 —4C **10**
Skelton Wlk. NN3 —3H **9**
Sketty Clo. NN4 —2H **21**
Skiddaw Wlk. NN3 —3H **9**
Skinners Hill. NN10 —3F **37**
Skipton Clo. NN4 —4A **20**
Sladeswell Ct. NN3 —1C **16**
Slater Clo. NN10 —3H **37**
Slipton Wlk. NN3 —2F **11**
Smithy, The. NN3 —6B **10**
Smyth Ct. NN3 —4B **10**
Snapewood Wlk. NN3 —3F **11**
Snetterton Clo. NN3 —3E **9**
Snowbell Sq. NN4 —4F **11**
Somerford Rd. NN8 —5G **27**
Somerset St. NN1 —2C **14**
Sotheby Rise. NN3 —4G **11**
Southampton Rd. NN4 —6B **14**
S. Bern. NN4 —6H **13**
S. Bridge Rd. NN4 —5C **14**
South Clo. NN10 —4G **37**
S. Copse. NN4 —4A **20**
Southcourt. NN3 —6G **3**
Southcrest. NN4 —2F **19**
Southern Relief Rd. NN1 —5B **14**
Southfield Av. NN4 —6C **14**
Southfield Rd. NN5 —2C **12**
Southfields. NN10 —4G **37**
Southfields Ho. NN3 —1D **10**
S. Holme Ct. NN3 —2B **10**
S. Oval. NN5 —6G **7**
S. Paddock Ct. NN3 —3C **10**
South Pk. NN10 —4F **37**
S. Portway Clo. NN3 —1C **10**
S. Priors Ct. NN3 —4D **10**
South St. NN1 —3E **15**
South Ter. NN1 —3E **15**
Southwood Hill. NN4 —1G **19**
Spanslade Rd. NN3 —6D **10**
Sparke Clo. NN8 —4F **27**
Spectacle La. NN3 —3E **3**
Spelhoe St. NN3 —1C **10**
Spencer Bri. Rd. NN5 —3H **13**
Spencer Clo. NN6 —5C **32**
Spencer Ct. NN2 —2E **37**
Spencer Haven. NN5 —2H **13**
Spencer Pde. NN1 —3C **14**
Spencer Rd. NN1 —2D **14**
Spencer Rd. NN9 —2C **30**
Spencer Rd. NN10 —1E **37**
Spencer St. NN5 —4H **13**
Spenfield Ct. NN3 —4C **10**
Spey Clo. NN8 —5E **27**
Spinney Clo. NN2 —6B **2**
Spinney Clo. NN10 —3D **36**
Spinney Dri. NN4 —1F **25**
Spinney Hill Cres. NN3 —3F **9**
Spinney Hill Rd. NN3 —3E **9**
Spinney Rd. NN3 —1G **9**
Spinney Rd. NN9 —1D **30**
Spinney Rd. NN10 —4D **36**
Spinneyside Wlk. NN3 —3D **10**
Spinney Ter. NN9 —1D **30**
Spinney Way. NN3 —2F **9**
Springbanks Way. NN4 —3A **20**

Spring Clo. NN2 —4B **2**
Springer Straight. NN4 —6G **13**
Springfield. NN3 —3H **15**
Springfield. NN4 —4D **20**
Springfield Ct. NN3 —4C **10**
Springfield Rd. NN10 —5G **37**
Springfield Rd. NN10 —4H **37**
Spring Gdns. NN1 —4C **14**
Spring Gdns. NN6 —5C **32**
Spring Gdns. NN8 —1H **33**
Spring Gdns. NN10 —5F **31**
Spring Ho. NN8 —1H **33**
(off Hill St.)
Spring Ho. NN8 —1H **33**
(off Wood St.)
Spring La. NN1 —3A **14**
Spring La. NN8 —1A **34**
Springs, The. NN4 —6H **13**
Spring St. NN9 —1D **30**
Springwood Ct. NN3 —2C **10**
Spruce Ct. NN3 —4B **10**
Spyglass Hill. NN4 —5A **20**
Square, The. NN6 —1B **2**
Squires Wlk. NN3 —4G **9**
Squirrel La. NN5 —2D **12**
Stable Ct. NN2 —4B **8**
Stafford Pl. NN3 —6E **3**
Stagshaw Clo. NN4 —3B **20**
Staines Clo. NN5 —3F **13**
Standens Barn Rd. NN3 —1C **16**
Stanfield Rd. NN5 —3D **12**
Stanford Way. NN4 —3B **20**
Stanhope Rd. NN2 —6B **8**
Stanley Rd. NN5 —3H **13**
Stanley Rd. NN8 —6B **28**
Stanley St. NN2 —1B **14**
Stanton Av. NN3 —3F **9**
Stanton Clo. NN8 —3B **28**
Stanwell Way. NN8 —2E **33**
Stanwick Rd. NN10 & NN9 —3G **31**
Starmers Yd. NN5 —2D **12**
Station Rd. NN3 —5F **11**
(in two parts)
Station Rd. NN6 —5B **32**
Station Rd. NN7 —4A **24**
(Blisworth)
Station Rd. NN7 —3G **17**
(Cogenhoe)
Station Rd. NN7 —5D **16**
(Little Houghton)
Station Rd. NN9 —1D **30**
(in two parts)
Station Rd. NN10 —3E **37**
Station Rd. NN29 —5H **35**
Steele Rd. NN8 —1F **33**
Steene St. NN5 —3H **13**
Stenson St. NN5 —3H **13**
Stephen Bennett Clo. NN5 —1D **12**
Stevens Clo. NN6 —4C **32**
Stevenson St. NN4 —1B **20**
Stewarts Rd. NN8 —2A **28**
Stimpson Av. NN1 —1E **15**
Stirling St. NN5 —2G **13**
Stockley St. NN1 —3D **14**
(in two parts)
Stockmead Rd. NN3 —1D **16**
Stocks Hill. NN3 —4H **3**
(off Cross St.)
Stockwell Av. NN4 —6C **20**
Stockwell Rd. NN7 —1C **24**
Stockwell Way. NN7 —1C **24**
Stoke Rd. NN7 —6A **24**
Stonebridge Ct. NN3 —4C **10**
Stonebridge La. NN9 —1C **26**
Stone Circ. Rd. NN3 —6B **4**
Stone Hill Ct. NN3 —3A **10**
Stonelea Rd. NN6 —2G **5**
Stoneleigh Chase. NN5 —6E **7**
Stone Way. NN5 —2C **12**
Stonewold Clo. NN2 —3H **7**
Stoneyhurst. NN4 —6G **13**
Stourhead Dri. NN4 —4B **20**
Stour Rd. NN5 —3G **13**
Stowe Wlk. NN3 —4G **9**
Stratford Dri. NN4 —5C **20**
Stratton Clo. NN3 —3A **16**
Strawberry Hill. NN3 —4F **11**
Straws Yd. NN9 —2C **30**

Streambank Rd. NN3 —1B **10**
Streatfield Rd. NN5 —1H **13**
Streeton Way. NN6 —4B **32**
Strelley Av. NN3 —1C **16**
Strode Rd. NN8 —6B **28**
Stuart Clo. NN4 —4G **19**
Stubble Clo. NN2 —1H **7**
Stubbs Clo. NN8 —4H **27**
Studland Rd. NN2 —6A **8**
Sulby Rd. NN3 —1B **10**
Sulgrave Rd. NN5 —2G **13**
Summerfields. NN4 —1F **19**
Summerhouse Rd. NN3 —1F **9**
Summit Rise. NN4 —4C **20**
Sunderland St. NN5 —3H **13**
Sundew Ct. NN4 —2E **19**
Sunningdale Clo. NN2 —5D **8**
Sunnyside. NN4 —5D **20**
Sunny Side. NN6 —5A **32**
Sunset Ct. NN3 —5D **10**
Sussex Clo. NN5 —3D **12**
Sutton Clo. NN2 —1C **8**
Swain Ct. NN3 —4B **10**
Swale Dri. NN5 —5G **7**
Swale Dri. NN8 —5E **27**
Swallow Clo. NN4 —4H **19**
Swallow Dri. NN10 —1F **37**
Swan La. NN8 —1A **34**
(off Midland Rd.)
Swansea Cres. NN5 —2H **13**
Swansea Rd. NN5 —1H **13**
Swanspool Ct. NN8 —1A **34**
Swanspool Pde. NN8 —2A **34**
Swan St. NN1 —4C **14**
Swan Yd. NN1 —3B **14**
Swinburne Rd. NN8 —1D **32**
Swinford Hollow. NN3 —1D **16**
Sycamore Clo. NN10 —3G **37**
Sycamore Rd. NN5 —2D **12**
Sylmond Gdns. NN10 —5D **36**
Sylvanus Rd. NN8 —6F **27**
Symington St. NN5 —2H **13**
Syresham Way. NN2 —2B **8**
Sywell Av. NN8 —5F **27**
Sywell Rd. NN4 —4C **4**
Sywell Rd. NN8 —5A **26**
Sywell Way. NN8 —5F **27**

Taborley Clo. NN3 —6C **10**
Talan Rise. NN3 —2E **11**
Talavera Way. NN3 —1H **9**
Talbot Rd. NN1 —2D **14**
Talbot Rd. NN8 —6C **28**
Talbot Rd. NN10 —4D **36**
Talbot Rd. N. NN8 —6C **28**
Tall Trees Clo. NN4 —3G **19**
Tallyfield End. NN4 —6F **13**
Tamar Clo. NN5 —5F **7**
Tamarish Dri. NN3 —1H **9**
Tanfield La. NN1 —4G **15**
Tanglewood. NN4 —1G **25**
Tanner St. NN1 —4B **14**
Tansy Clo. NN4 —2E **19**
Tapeley Gdns. NN4 —4C **20**
Tarn Croft. NN3 —4G **9**
Tarragon Way. NN4 —5C **20**
Tarrant Clo. NN3 —4A **4**
Tarrant Way. NN3 —4A **4**
Tate Gro. NN4 —4D **20**
Tattersall Clo. NN3 —3F **9**
Taunton Av. NN3 —2H **15**
Tavistock Clo. NN3 —5G **11**
Taylor Clo. NN8 —4E **27**
Teal Clo. NN4 —3E **19**
Teal La. NN8 —4B **28**
Tebbutt's Dri. NN6 —5B **32**
Tees Clo. NN8 —5E **27**
Teesdale. NN3 —1C **10**
Templar Dri. NN2 —3H **7**
Temple Bar. NN1 —2B **14**
Tenby Rd. NN5 —1H **13**
Tennyson Clo. NN5 —1G **13**
Tennyson Rd. NN8 —2F **33**
Tennyson Rd. NN10 —3D **36**
Ten Pines. NN3 —6C **4**
Tenter Clo. NN10 —6F **31**
Tenter Rd. NN3 —6E **3**

Teviot Clo. NN5 —5F **7**
Tewkesbury Clo. NN8 —5F **27**
Thames Rd. NN4 —4B **20**
Thames Rd. NN8 —5E **27**
Thatchwell Ct. NN3 —1C **16**
Thebwell Rd. NN3 —6C **10**
Thenford St. NN1 —3D **14**
Third Av. NN8 —2F **33**
Thirlestane Cres. NN4 —6A **14**
Thirlestane Rd. NN4 —6A **14**
Thirlmere Av. NN3 —4H **9**
Thistle Ct. NN4 —6H **13**
Thistleholme Clo. NN2 —4D **8**
Thomas Flawn Rd. NN9 —3B **30**
Thomas St. NN1 —2C **14**
(off Bailiff St.)
Thomas St. NN8 —6B **28**
Thorburn Rd. NN3 —1B **16**
Thornapple Clo. NN3 —3F **11**
Thornby Dri. NN2 —4A **8**
Thornfield. NN3 —3F **11**
Thorn Hill. NN4 —6G **13**
Thornton Rd. NN2 —6A **8**
Thorpe Clo. NN8 —6E **27**
Thorpe Rd. NN4 —6B **14**
Thorpe Rd. NN6 —6A **32**
Thorpeville. NN3 —6A **4**
Three Mile Wlk. NN3 —4F **11**
Thrift St. NN10 —6F **31**
Thrift St. NN29 —5G **35**
Thrush La. NN8 —5B **28**
Thruxton Dri. NN3 —3E **9**
Thursby Rd. NN1 —2G **15**
Thurspit Pl. NN3 —5G **11**
Thwaite Wlk. NN3 —6D **10**
Thyme Ct. NN3 —4B **10**
Tideswell Clo. NN4 —3G **19**
Tiffany Gdns. NN4 —5B **20**
Tinsley Clo. NN3 —4E **11**
Tintagel Clo. NN10 —5H **37**
Tintern Av. NN5 —2H **13**
Tiptoe Clo. NN3 —3F **11**
Tithe Barn Rd. NN8 —1A **34**
Titley Bawk Av. NN6 —3C **32**
Tiverton Av. NN2 —6B **2**
Tollbar. NN10 —6F **31**
Tollgate Clo. NN2 —5A **8**
Tollgate Way. NN5 —3E **13**
Tom's Clo. NN4 —2F **25**
Tonmead Rd. NN3 —3B **10**
Tonmead Wlk. NN3 —4B **10**
Top Meadow Wlk. NN3 —4D **10**
Topwell Ct. NN3 —6C **10**
Torrington Cres. NN8 —5G **27**
Torrington Grn. NN8 —6G **27**
Torrington Rd. NN8 —5G **27**
Torrington Way. NN8 —5G **27**
Towcester Rd. NN7 & NN4 —3B **24**
Tower Field Sq. NN3 —1D **10**
Tower St. NN1 —3B **14**
Townley Way. NN6 —4B **32**
Townsend Clo. NN8 —1H **33**
Townwell La. NN29 —5H **35**
Trafford Rd. NN10 —3G **37**
Treetops. NN3 —2D **10**
Treetops. NN4 —6D **20**
Trelawney. NN8 —6D **26**
Trent Clo. NN5 —5F **7**
Trent Clo. NN8 —5E **27**
Tresham Grn. NN8 —6E **7**
Trevor Clo. NN5 —2F **13**
Trevor Cres. NN5 —2F **13**
Trimley Clo. NN3 —3A **16**
Trinity Av. NN2 —6C **8**
Trinity Cen. NN4 —4C **26**
Triumph Gdns. NN5 —1A **12**
Trojan Cen. NN8 —3A **28**
Troon Cres. NN8 —4E **27**
Troutbeck Wlk. NN3 —3H **9**
Trussell Rd. NN3 —6F **11**
Tudor Rd. NN1 —5F **9**
Tudor Way. NN8 —4G **27**
Turnby Ct. NN8 —4E **27**
Turnells Mill La. NN8 —3B **34**
Turnells Mill Rd. NN8 —4A **34**
Turner Rd. NN8 —4H **27**
Turner St. NN1 —2E **15**
Turn Furlong. NN2 —2H **7**

Tweed Rd. NN5 —4E **13**
Twyford Clo. NN3 —1D **16**
Tyebeck Ct. NN2 —4A **8**
Tyes Ct. NN3 —4C **10**
Tyne Clo. NN8 —5E **27**
Tyne Rd. NN5 —3F **13**
Tyringham Clo. NN3 —6A **10**

Ullswater Clo. NN8 —6E **27**
Underbank La. NN3 —1H **9**
Upland Rd. NN3 —5H **9**
Up. Cross St. NN1 —3B **14**
Up. Havelock St. NN8 —6A **28**
Up. Kings Av. NN10 —4G **31**
Up. Mounts. NN1 —3C **14**
Up. Park Av. NN10 —4D **36**
Up. Priory St. NN1 —2B **14**
Up. Queen St. NN10 —2G **37**
Up. Thrift St. NN1 —3E **15**
Uppingham St. NN1 —2A **14**
Upton Clo. NN2 —1C **8**
Upton Way. NN5 —4E **13**
Usher Ho. NN2 —2C **8**

Valemead Wlk. NN3 —3D **10**
Valentine Way. NN3 —4F **11**
Vale, The. NN1 —6F **9**
Valley Cres. NN3 —6E **11**
Valley Rd. NN3 —6E **11**
Valley Rd. NN8 —3H **33**
Vantage Meadow. NN3 —4G **11**
Vardon Clo. NN8 —4E **27**
Vaux Rd. NN8 —2A **28**
Velocette Way. NN5 —6A **6**
Verdant Vale. NN4 —5C **20**
Vernon St. NN1 —3E **15**
Vernon Ter. NN1 —3E **15**
Vernon Wlk. NN1 —3E **15**
Verwood Clo. NN3 —2C **10**
Vicarage Clo. NN2 —4H **7**
Vicarage Clo. NN8 —5F **27**
Vicarage Farm Rd. NN8 —5F **27**
Vicarage La. NN2 —4H **7**
Vicarage Rd. NN5 —2H **13**
Victoria Clo. NN6 —4B **32**
Victoria Clo. NN10 —2F **37**
Victoria Ct. NN3 —1F **11**
Victoria Gdns. NN1 —4C **14**
Victoria Pk. NN8 —3B **34**
Victoria Promenade. NN1 —4C **14**
Victoria Rd. NN1 —3D **14**
Victoria Rd. NN7 —4H **17**
Victoria Rd. NN8 —1A **34**
Victoria Rd. NN10 —2F **37**
Victoria St. NN1 —3C **14**
Victoria St. NN6 —4C **32**
Victoria St. NN10 —2C **30**
Vienne Clo. NN5 —1A **12**
Vigo Cres. NN1 —4D **14**
Vigo Ter. NN1 —4D **14**
Vincent Clo. NN5 —1A **12**
Vine Hill Clo. NN10 —5E **31**
Vine Hill Dri. NN10 —5F **31**
Viscount Rd. NN3 —1F **11**
Vivian Rd. NN8 —6B **28**
Vokes Clo. NN3 —6D **10**
Vyse Rd. NN2 —6A **2**

Wade Meadow Ct. NN3 —3C **10**
Wade Meadow Wlk. NN3 —4C **10**
Wagtail Clo. NN3 —6H **3**
Waingrove. NN3 —3E **11**
Wakefield. NN8 —1E **33**
Wakefield Rd. NN2 —3C **8**
Wakehurst Dri. NN4 —4B **20**
Walgrave Clo. NN8 —1E **17**
Walker Sq. NN8 —4E **27**
Wallace Gdns. NN2 —5E **9**
Wallace Rd. NN2 —5E **9**
Wallace Ter. NN2 —5E **9**
Wallbeck Clo. NN2 —3B **8**
Walledwell Ct. NN3 —6C **10**
Wallingford End. NN3 —1D **16**
Wallis Clo. NN8 —1C **32**
Walmer Clo. NN10 —4H **37**

Walton Heath Way. NN2 —4D **8**
Wansford Wlk. NN3 —1B **10**
Wantage Clo. NN3 —4B **4**
Wantage Rd. NN1 —1F **15**
Wantage Rd. NN29 —5H **35**
Wardington Ct. NN2 —3A **8**
Wardlow Clo. NN4 —3G **19**
Warmonds Hill. NN10 —6F **31**
Warnham. NN8 —6D **26**
Warren Clo. NN29 —6A **36**
Warren Rd. NN5 —2G **13**
Warrens Clo. NN9 —1D **30**
Warren, The. NN4 —3E **21**
Warwick Clo. NN5 —1C **12**
Warwick Rd. NN8 —3A **34**
Washbrook Clo. NN3 —6E **11**
Washbrook La. NN6 —2H **11**
Washbrook Rd. NN10 —2E **37**
Washington St. NN4 —4A **8**
Waterfowl Wlk. NN3 —6E **11**
Watering La. NN4 —1F **25**
Water La. NN4 —5D **20**
Waterloo Rd. NN8 —1H **33**
Watermeadow Dri. NN3 —2C **10**
Waterpump Ct. NN3 —2B **10**
Watersmeet. NN1 —3G **15**
Waterview Wlk. NN3 —2B **10**
Waterworks La. NN8 —4E **27**
Watkin Ter. NN1 —2C **14**
Watson Clo. NN8 —4E **27**
Waveney Way. NN5 —6G **7**
Waverley Rd. NN2 —6D **8**
Waypost Ct. NN3 —4C **10**
Wayside Acres. NN4 —3A **20**
Weavers Rd. NN8 —1F **33**
Weavers, The. NN4 —4B **20**
Weddell Way. NN4 —1H **21**
Wedmore Clo. NN5 —2E **13**
Weedon Rd. NN7 & NN5 —4A **12**
Weggs Farm Rd. NN5 —1A **12**
Weir Clo. NN8 —5H **27**
Weldon Clo. NN4 —4F **27**
Welford Rd. NN2 —1G **7**
Welland Grn. NN5 —5G **7**
Welland Wlk. NN5 —5G **7**
Welland Way. NN5 —5G **7**
Wellingborough Rd. NN1, NN3 & NN6
—3D **14**
Wellingborough Rd. NN6 —4C **32**
(Earls Barton)
Wellingborough Rd. NN6 —3H **11**
(Ecton)
Wellingborough Rd. NN6 —2H **5**
(Sywell)
Wellingborough Rd. NN8 & NN9
—3D **28**
Wellingborough Rd. NN9 —1G **27**
(Great Harrowden)
Wellingborough Rd. NN9 —4H **29**
(Irthlingborough)
Wellingborough Rd. NN10 —2B **36**
Wellington St. NN1 —3C **14**
Wells Ct. NN8 —3C **8**
Well Spring. NN7 —6A **24**
Well Yd. NN2 —4A **8**
Wenlock Way. NN5 —1E **13**
Wensleydale. NN2 —2G **7**
Wentworth Av. NN8 —5E **27**

Wentworth Rd. NN10 —3E **37**
Wentworth Way. NN2 —4D **8**
Wessex Way. NN3 —6G **9**
West Bank. NN3 —1B **10**
West Brook. NN7 —5A **24**
Westbrook. NN8 —1D **32**
Westbury Clo. NN5 —2E **13**
Westcott Way. NN3 —2A **16**
West Cres. NN10 —3C **36**
Westerdale. NN2 —2G **7**
Western View. NN1 —4A **14**
Western Way. NN8 —2F **33**
Westfield Av. NN10 —3C **36**
Westfield Rd. NN5 —1C **12**
(Duston)
Westfield Rd. NN5 —3G **13**
(Northampton)
Westfield Rd. NN8 —1G **33**
Westfields Av. NN10 —6F **31**
Westfields St. NN10 —6F **31**
Westfields Ter. NN10 —6F **31**
Westlea Rd. NN6 —2G **5**
W. Leys Ct. NN3 —6H **3**
W. Mead Ct. NN3 —6C **10**
Westminster Rd. NN8 —4F **27**
Westone Av. NN3 —6A **10**
Weston Favell Cen. NN3 —5C **10**
Weston Mill La. NN3 —2B **16**
Weston Way. NN3 —1H **15**
Weston Wharf. NN1 —4B **14**
W. Oval. NN5 —6G **7**
W. Paddock Ct. NN3 —3C **10**
W. Priors Ct. NN3 —3C **10**
W. Ridge. NN2 —4C **8**
W. Rising. NN4 —4C **20**
West St. NN1 —3E **15**
West St. NN3 —4G **3**
West St. NN6 —5A **32**
(Earls Barton)
West St. NN6 —4H **11**
(Ecton)
West St. NN8 —1H **33**
West St. NN10 —3F **37**
West View. NN8 —4C **34**
W. Villa Cotts. NN8 —1H **33**
W. Villa Rd. NN8 —1H **33**
West Way. NN6 —4A **32**
Wetheral Clo. NN3 —3H **9**
Whaddon Clo. NN4 —2F **19**
Whalley Gro. NN7 —3H **17**
Wharfe Grn. NN5 —5G **7**
Wharf Rd. NN10 —5E **31**
Wheatcroft Gdns. NN10 —3F **37**
Wheatfield Gdns. NN3 —6G **9**
Wheatfield Rd. NN3 —5G **9**
Wheatfield Rd. S. NN3 —6G **9**
Wheatfield Ter. NN3 —6G **9**
Whernside. NN8 —5F **27**
Whernside Way. NN5 —1D **12**
Whilton Rd. NN2 —3C **8**
Whistlets Clo. NN4 —2E **19**
Whiston Rd. NN2 —3C **8**
White Delves. NN8 —4G **27**
White Doe Dri. NN3 —6H **3**
Whitefield Rd. NN5 —6C **6**
Whitefriars. NN10 —4C **36**
Whitegates. NN4 —2E **19**

Whiteheart Clo. NN3 —5E **11**
Whitehills Cres. NN2 —1A **8**
Whitehills Way. NN2 —1A **8**
Whiteland Rd. NN3 —5H **9**
White Way. NN6 —4B **32**
Whitfield Way. NN2 —2C **8**
Whiting Ct. NN3 —5H **3**
Whittemore Rd. NN10 —2H **37**
Whittlebury Clo. NN2 —2C **8**
Whittle Clo. NN8 —5D **26**
Whitworth Cres. NN6 —4B **32**
Whitworth Rd. NN1 —2E **15**
Whitworth Rd. NN8 —6C **28**
Whitworth Way. NN8 —3B **34**
Whitworth Way. NN9 —3C **30**
Whytewell Rd. NN8 —5H **27**
Wilberforce St. NN1 —3D **14**
Wilbye Grange. NN8 —3F **33**
Wilby La. NN29 —6F **33**
Wilby St. NN1 —3E **15**
Wilby Way. NN8 —3F **33**
Wildacre Rd. NN10 —3C **36**
Wildern La. NN4 —6B **20**
Wilford Av. NN3 —1C **16**
William St. NN1 —2C **14**
William Trigg Clo. NN9 —3C **30**
Williton Clo. NN3 —2A **16**
Willow Brook Sq. NN3 —4G **11**
Willow Cres. NN4 —1B **22**
Willow La. NN4 —1B **22**
Willow Rise. NN3 —1E **17**
Willows, The. NN4 —5G **15**
Wilson Cres. NN9 —2C **30**
Wilson Rd. NN10 —3E **37**
Wilson Way. NN6 —6B **32**
Wimbledon St. NN5 —3H **13**
Wimborne Clo. NN3 —4G **11**
Wimpole. NN8 —1E **33**
Winchester Clo. NN4 —2B **20**
Winchester Rd. NN4 —2B **20**
Winchester Rd. NN10 —4G **37**
Windermere Dri. NN8 —6E **27**
Windermere Way. NN3 —3H **9**
Windflower Pl. NN3 —5G **11**
Windingbrook La. NN4 —6B **20**
Windmill Av. NN7 —6A **24**
Windmill Banks. NN10 —4F **31**
Windmill Clo. NN8 —3G **33**
Windmill Rd. NN9 —2C **30**
Windmill Rd. NN10 —3E **37**
Windmill Ter. NN2 —2C **8**
Windrush Rd. NN4 —3E **21**
Windrush Way. NN5 —6H **7**
Windsor Cr. NN3 —5F **11**
Windsor Cres. NN5 —3F **13**
Windsor Ho. NN5 —1D **12**
Windsor Rd. NN8 —4G **33**
Windsor Rd. NN10 —2G **37**
Windyridge. NN2 —4C **8**
Winnington Clo. NN3 —2F **11**
Winsford Way. NN3 —2A **16**
Winstanley Rd. NN8 —1B **34**
Winston Clo. NN3 —2H **9**
Wisley Clo. NN4 —4B **20**
Witham Grn. NN5 —5F **7**
Witham Wlk. NN5 —5G **7**
Witham Way. NN5 —6G **7**
Witton Rd. NN5 —1D **12**

Woburn Ct. NN10 —5E **37**
Woburn Ga. NN3 —4G **11**
Wollaston Rd. NN29 —6F **35**
Wollaton Gdns. NN3 —1C **16**
Woodavens Clo. NN4 —2E **19**
Woodborough Gdns. NN3 —1B **16**
Woodcote Av. NN3 —3E **9**
Woodfields Wlk. NN3 —2B **10**
Woodford St. NN1 —3D **14**
Woodford Wlk. NN1 —3D 14
(off Woodford St.)
Woodhall Clo. NN4 —2E **19**
Wood Hill. NN1 —4C **14**
Woodhill Rd. NN5 —6C **6**
Woodland Av. NN3 —6F **9**
Woodland Av. NN6 —4E **5**
Woodland Clo. NN5 —5C **6**
Woodland Rd. NN10 —2E **37**
Woodlands Rd. NN29 —6F **35**
Woodley Chase. NN5 —6C **6**
Woodpecker Way. NN4 —4G **19**
Woodrush Way. NN3 —6H **3**
Woodside Av. NN3 —3A **10**
Woodside Cres. NN3 —3A **10**
Woodside Grn. NN5 —6G **7**
Woodside Wlk. NN5 —6F **7**
Woodside Way. NN5 —6F **7**
Woodstock. NN1 —3E **15**
Woodstock Clo. NN8 —4G **27**
Wood St. NN8 —1H **33**
Wood St. NN10 —6G **31**
Woolmonger St. NN1 —4B **14**
Wootton Brook Clo. NN4 —5B **20**
Wootton Hall Pk. NN4 —3C **20**
Wootton Hill Farm. NN4 —3G **19**
Worcester Clo. NN3 —5E **11**
Wordsworth Rd. NN8 —2D **32**
Wrenbury Rd. NN5 —1A **12**
Wrenbury Rd. W. NN5 —1A **12**
Wychwood Clo. NN5 —6B **6**
Wycliffe Rd. NN1 —2F **15**
Wye Clo. NN8 —5E **27**
Wykeham Rd. NN10 —4G **31**
Wymersley Clo. NN4 —1C **22**
Wymington Pk. NN10 —4F **37**
Wymington Rd. NN10 —6F **37**
Wysall Rd. NN3 —2D **10**

Yardley Dri. NN2 —1C **8**
Yarrow. NN8 —2D **32**
Yarwell Sq. NN4 —1G **19**
Yeldon Ct. NN8 —2B **28**
Yelvertoft Rd. NN4 —4B **8**
Yeoman Dri. NN2 —2A **8**
Yeoman Meadow. NN4 —3G **19**
Yewtree Ct. NN3 —2A **10**
York Av. NN7 —3H **17**
York Clo. NN10 —4G **31**
York Rd. NN1 —3C **14**
York Rd. NN8 —6B **28**
York Rd. NN10 —4G **31**
(Higham Ferrers)
York Rd. NN10 —4G **37**
(Rushden)